# Looking Past the Sky

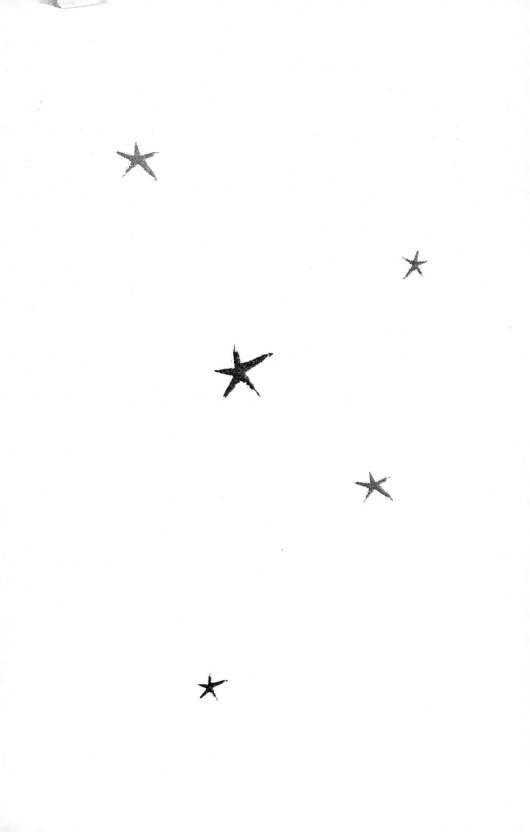

# Looking Past the Sky

## Prayers by Young Teens

Edited by Marilyn Kielbasa

Saint Mary's Press®

Genuine recycled paper with 10% post-consumer waste.

The publishing team included Marilyn Kielbasa, development editor; Laurie A. Berg, copy editor; James H. Gurley, production editor; Hollace Storkel, typesetter; Maurine R. Twait, art director; Cindi Ramm, cover designer; pre-press, printing, and binding by the graphics division of Saint Mary's Press.

The scriptural quotations in this book are from the New Revised Standard Version of the Bible. Copyright © 1989 by the Division of Christian Education of the National Council of the Churches of Christ in the United States of America. All rights reserved.

Printed in the United States of America

Printing: 6 5 4 3

Year: 2007 06 05

ISBN 0-88489-582-3

# Contents

# Preface

In the summer of 1997, Saint Mary's Press, in Winona, Minnesota, hosted a focus group on early adolescence. We invited nine people from around the country who work with young people ages eleven to fifteen. These people were catechists, youth ministers, diocesan personnel, schoolteachers, and counselors. One of the strongest recommendations that came from the group was to do a book of prayers by young teens, similar to *Dreams Alive* and *More Dreams Alive*. Both of those collections of prayers by teenagers, published by Saint Mary's Press in 1991 and 1995 respectively, have been popular with young people and with those who work with young people.

In October 1997, I sent a letter to parish and diocesan religious education offices, youth ministry offices, and parochial elementary and middle schools all over North America. The letter was an invitation to collect prayers by young people in the sixth, seventh, and eighth grades and submit them for possible publication. No topics were specified. The prayers could be funny or serious, and could be focused on the young people themselves, on other people, or on the bigger picture. Most important, the guidelines indicated that "we are looking for writing that reflects honesty, authenticity, and an awareness of the real world of young adolescents."

The writers were given the option of being identified by their full name, their first name, or their initials, or of remaining anonymous. All prayers were identified by the school or parish from which they came.

Because this project was directed at a relatively new audience for Saint Mary's Press, I was not quite sure what to expect. I was pleasantly astounded by the response. Prayers and reflections poured in from all over the country; by the end of February 1998, we had collected over fourteen hundred prayers by young adolescents from forty-three states, the District of Columbia, the Virgin Islands, and Guam.

Though the response surprised me, the quality of the prayers did not. They were honest, thoughtful, humorous, sincere, reflective, joyful, sensitive, passionate, anguished, fun, touching—in other words, they reflected the spectrum of life.

On more than one occasion, I was moved to prayer myself, inspired by something one of the young teens had written. Most of the editing process was done in awesome wonder, with the words of the Scriptures echoing in my mind and heart: "And a . . . child shall lead them" (Isaiah 11:6).

The most difficult aspect of editing this book was having to eliminate so many wonderful prayers. The task of choosing the prayers and reflections was, at times, agonizing. Thankfully, I had help. After reading and sorting all the prayers, I asked six students to read through them and give me feedback. The team included Christopher Gorman and Julie Rozek, from Winona Senior High School and Saint Mary's Parish; and Gretchen Baumgardt, John Corcoran, Ryan Hinton, and Ruth Kolar, from Saint Mary's University of Minnesota, in Winona, Minnesota.

I am sure the students would agree with me that the assignment was a difficult one. However, the contribution of this student advisory team was indispensable, and I am grateful to them for their help.

## Using the Prayers

The prayers and reflections in this book are useful to young people individually, as well as in ministry settings and family settings. The uses are too numerous to list, but some suggestions follow:

- Adults who work with young adolescents in ministry settings might consider using the prayers in these ways:
  - to start or end a class
  - to give focus to a prayer session
  - as part of a retreat
  - to trigger discussion about topics of importance to young teens
  - as part of parent, sponsor, or staff meetings
- *Looking Past the Sky* would be a helpful gift to parents and to adults who work with young teens in secular settings. The prayers can remind adults that young adolescents are people of faith. Young teens' age and place in life give them a unique perspective on God, the world, relationships, and themselves.

- Young people can use the book in these ways:
  - for personal prayer in the morning, in the evening, or anytime in between
  - as a springboard to write their own prayers or reflections in a personal journal
  - to share with friends or family members

The uses of *Looking Past the Sky* are limited only by one's creativity. If you find a unique way to use this book, I would love to hear about it. Write to Marilyn Kielbasa at Saint Mary's Press, 702 Terrace Heights, Winona, MN 55987-1320. My e-mail address is *mkielbasa@smp.org.*

## A Final Word of Thanks

A book like this would not be possible without the contributions and cooperation of many people:

- Thanks to the diocesan, parish, and school personnel who got the word out, gathered the prayers, and submitted them.
- Thanks to parents, catechists, and teachers who nurture the faith of young people in families, parishes, and schools.
- Thanks to the young people themselves who allowed their prayers and reflections to be submitted for consideration. I only wish we could have published all of them.

*Looking Past the Sky* is a collection of prayerful thoughts of young people—who are the present and the future of the world and the church. My wish is that every person who opens this book finds in it consolation, inspiration, and great hope.

*Marilyn Kielbasa*
*Editor*

# Part One

# Prayers to Begin and End the Day

Promise to God

Thank you for guiding me t' you

In the name of the Father, protect
In the name of the Son, help me
of the Holy Spirit, & I m
r way.

Angel of God protect me throughout the
me of any harm, fear, or evil that stands in
disturbs my connection with God.

Dear Lord,
Help me through my day,
May it go by safe and easy.
AMEN

my family and friends
have a successful

# Morning Prayers

★★★

Good morning, God. It's me.
I see my eyes are open,
The sun is shining.
I can't think of one bad thing.
For right now, the world is right.
Please let this day continue this way.
Guide me, watch over me, bless me.
Thank you, God. I love you, God.
Amen.

*Aaron Orlando*
*Saint Ambrose School, Houston, TX*


★★★

Dear God,
Help me through this day,
Through the good times and the bad times that come my
        way.
I need help on that gigantic test,
The spelling, the science, and all the rest.
I need help with the problems that lie ahead.
God, help me through the times when I just want to go
        to bed.
And when I go to bed tonight, I'll be sure and pray.
But please, dear God, help me get through today.
Amen.

*Megan Borer*
*Saint Thomas More School, Omaha, NE*

Dear God,
I beg of you to guide me through the troubles that will face me this day. Please help me with the prayers and petitions I give you, that you may hear me in my despair. I turn to you for answers when I am confused, and you are there to help me decide what to do. If it's a worldly-known problem or just a minor glitch at home, no problem is too big or too small for you. That is why you are our God. Once again, I turn to you this day for the guidance and hope to make it through yet another day. Amen.

*Anthony Capizzi*
*Saint Cyprian School, Sunnyvale, CA*

Dear God,
Thank you for giving me life, for waking me up, and for giving me the gift of another day. Help me to see the good in other people and to do what is right for the sake of others. Help other people to see what is right, and help them to do no evil. Give me the gift of love, laughter, and everlasting peace. Amen.

*Emily Hamer*
*Saint Joseph School, Wauwatosa, WI*

Our Lord my God, I want to give you thanks for the wonderful day you have given us and for letting me live another day. Make my day peaceful, and let no evil take over me. I praise you, my God. Amen.

*Candina Rodriguez*
*Our Lady of Lourdes Parish, Violet, LA*

God, today, keep me in your thoughts.
Help me to remember the value
Of things that cannot be sold or bought,
Like love, honesty, courage, and kindness,
And all other things you taught.
I offer my day to you, O God,
So keep me in your thoughts.

*Kelly Koeninger*
*Saint Thomas School, Fort Thomas, KY*

O Lord God on high,
We are thankful for this day; help us to use it wisely.
Help us to teach those who cannot learn,
Help us to feed those who cannot support themselves,
Help us to pray for those who do not believe in you,
Help us to be kind to those who are unhappy,
Help us to always look for you and keep seeking you.
This we ask through Jesus Christ, our Savior. Amen.

*Christopher Navarro Mahoney*
*Saint Ambrose School, Houston, TX*

Please help me get through the day
and not worry what others say.
I can quickly get very upset.
I hate being so sensitive.
So please help me keep calm
and not worry about everything and everyone.

*Kathryn Elizabeth Klein*
*Holy Spirit School, Louisville, KY*

As the sun peeks through my window,
I wake each morning knowing that you are near.
I rise from my bed and bow low.
I pray silently to you, knowing that you will hear.
I ask that you help me face the day.
I ask that you keep safe my family and friends.
I know that you will, for "no" you never say.
And when the day has drawn to an end,
I will climb back into my bed.
My room will fill with moonlight,
And I will think of all that you have said,
Knowing that you will keep me in your sight.

*Kelly McGrath*
*Our Lady of Hope/Saint Luke School, Baltimore, MD*

In the name of the **Father**, protect my family and friends.

In the name of the **Son**, help me to have a successful day.

In the name of the **Holy Spirit**, help kindness grow in

the world.

Amen.

*Roger Priego*
*Saint Bartholomew School, Bethesda, MD*

**Angel of God**, protect me throughout the day.
Protect me from any harm, fear, or evil that stands in my
path or disturbs my connection with God. Amen.

*David J. Atkins*
*Saint Pius X School, Tulsa, OK*

Dear God,
Thank you for putting a smile on my face and a warm special feeling in my mind, heart, and soul today.

Some days it's hard to be around other people when they hurt my feelings. But sooner or later, your love will shine through them.

Be with me so that I can have the strength and courage to make the right choices. Amen.

*Michael*
*Saint Richard Catholic Community, Richfield, MN*

In the name of the Father, please guide and protect me
    throughout the day.
In the name of the Son, thank you, Jesus, for dying for us on
    the cross and for showing us the path for a sinless life.
In the name of the Holy Spirit, thank you for always being
    there in my times of need. Amen.

*M. K.*
*Saint Bartholomew School, Bethesda, MD*

# Evening Prayers

Dear God, creator of heaven and earth,
Thank you for this wonderful day,
For all the cool things I have received.
Please bless my mom, dad, brothers, sisters, grandma and
grandpa, aunts, uncles, and cousins,
The poor and the homeless.
Please try to bring justice and peace to the earth.
God, have a great night.
When it is my time, please make it peaceful.
Amen.

*Matt Schueller*
*Saint Joseph School, Wauwatosa, WI*


Dear God, Mary, and Jesus,
I just want to say thank you for this wonderful day with my
friends, my family, and at school.
I am sorry for all the sins I have committed today.
I offer a prayer for my nanny;
Help her get through everything.
I pray for myself, that I may have a good day tomorrow;
For my mother, father, brother, and anyone in the world who
needs help and love.
Thank you, God, for everything you have given me today
and always!
Amen.

*Corinne Hartin*
*Sacred Heart School, Bayside, NY*

Thank you, God,
For this whole day.
Thank you, God,
For all the play.
Thank you, God,
For all I say.
Thank you, God,
In every way.

*Alexandra Portolano*
*Saint Andrew the Apostle Parish, Silver Spring, MD*

God,
Today was a beautiful day. The sky was blue, and the sun was
shining. I woke up on time and fully rested. I gave my mom
and dad a kiss and left for school. When I got to school,
I even had extra time to talk to my friends. My teachers were
in good moods, and I received an A plus on my test. I didn't
even have that much homework. My mom came home at
five o'clock and I helped her start dinner. My dad came
home at six fifteen. I greeted him with a hug. We finished
eating, and I cleared off the table. I read for a little bit, then
got ready for bed. Now I am talking to you. Thank you for
everything today. I was wondering if you could watch over
my mom, my dad, my brothers, all my friends, and especially
my aunts and those who aren't as fortunate as I am. Also,
if you could help me during my test tomorrow, I would
appreciate it. I know that I don't always do what's right, but
tomorrow is another day, and I will try harder. Thank you for
everything you have given me. I love you. Amen.

*Katrina Gatta*
*Holy Rosary School, Claymont, DE*

Dear God,
Please protect my family and relatives. Keep me safe from evil and danger in my sleep and while I'm awake. Forgive me for all I have done wrong. Help the people I have hurt or treated unfairly to forgive me. Thank you for the many gifts you have given me. Guide me to do the right things. Help me to become more like you. Goodnight, God. I love you.

*Bernardine Coughlin*
*Saint John Vianney School, Saint Pete Beach, FL*

Dear God,
Thank you for everything you gave me today. Thank you for my family. They mean a lot to me. I am sorry for everything I did wrong today. I just wanted to say thank you for loving me each and every day. I love you! Amen.

*Lauren Spittler*
*Saint Vincent de Paul School, Omaha, NE*

Dear God,
Thank you for a great day. Thank you for not letting anything bad happen to my family. Please let us have a safe night. Please don't let anything bad happen. If something bad has to happen, let it happen to me. Please forgive me for all the wrong I did during the day. Please make sure I wake up in the morning, and help me through tomorrow. Please protect me when I am scared. Please let my mom get home safely from work. Thank you, God, for everything. I love you. Amen.

*Bernadette*
*Saint John Vianney School, Saint Pete Beach, FL*

Dear God,

Help me through my day.

May it go by *safe* and *easy.*

Amen.

*Kyle Dean Davis*
*Saint Francis de Sales Parish, Lebanon, MO*


Thank you for guiding me through this day.
I pray with **all my heart** I may
Teach others to follow in your way.

*Renee M. Thibodeau*
*Saint Louis School of Religion, Fort Kent, ME*

Dear God,
Hello! It is me again. I was looking at the stars, and I realized what a good job you did! They sparkle like diamonds in the night. Thank you for my family and friends. Without them I would be next to nothing. Thank you for all the animals and plants. Please help those who are sick and dying and their families and friends. Please help me control my temper and be nicer to other people.

I am sorry for yelling at people that shouldn't be yelled at. I am also especially sorry for bugging my parents. Please forgive me. Well, that's all for now. Thanks for listening. I love you.

*Michelle L. Ciesielski*
*Saint Agnes School, Springfield, MO*

Dear God, forgive me for the sins I have committed today.
Help me to sin less and to become more and more like you.
Help me to resist evil and all temptations in my life.
Help me to have more patience and tolerance toward others.
Most of all, help me to love others as you have loved me.
Amen.

*Kathryn Wilson*
*Saint John Kanty School, Milwaukee, WI*

God, I thought of you today
when I slept and when I played.
God, I thought of you today
when I saw the birds and trees,
when I saw the flowers bloom,
when I saw the bee get honey,
when my dog chewed his bone,
when my cat stubbed her toe.
God, I think of you every day,
but most of all today.

*Laura Hausladen*
*Saint Paul School, Saint Paul, MO*

Dear God,
We're sorry for all the wrong things we did today. As we
think back on doing those bad things, it just doesn't seem
like they were even worth the effort anymore. Even though
our evil may show through our actions, we still have enough
love in our heart to try to turn our wrongs into rights. Please
help us do better tomorrow. Amen.

*Brigid Mullen*
*Saint John the Baptist School, Howard, WI*

★ ★ ★

Dear God,
Thank you for this day. Thank you for letting me go to school and come home again. Thank you for my family. I thank you for letting me eat my three meals today. And thank you, God, for everything around me. Amen.

*Andrew W. Repasky*
*Saint Elizabeth Ann Seton Parish, Fort Collins, CO*


★ ★ ★

God, as I sleep through the night,
I know that you will keep me safe.
As I walk through the day,
I know that you are near my heart.
As you lead me and guide me,
I learn right from wrong.
And when I say my nightly prayers,
I know that you will be there for me tomorrow.
Amen.

*Wendy Ponze*
*Saint Catherine of Siena School, Metairie, LA*


★ ★ ★

Dear God,
Thank you for another day. Thank you for life, for friends, and for everything you give me. I pray that I may always live out your will. I pray, too, for the people who sacrifice their life for freedom and justice.

*Jaemi Bowers*
*Saint Theresa School, Phoenix, AZ*

# Part Two

# Thank You, God

hank you for _____ oug

Please God, watch over me _____ ays;
whatever I do
_____herever I
_____us, & whatever
_____e guide _____

O Lord
Help me with life
Help me choose what i_
Show me the _____

lots of things t_
_____d times +

In the name of the Father, protect
In the name of the Son, help me
_____ name of the Holy Spirit, _____
Amen.

Dear Lord,
You tell us to make pea_
with others, but sometimes it_
hard. You help us in times _
need. Help us to love others a_
_sus said.

_____ because it can
_____ and so can
_____ help me with

Creator of the earth:

I like to thank you for all the things that you have given to us
without our asking, like the flowers that show us their
smiling faces—the yellow flowers of thousand petals.

I give you thanks for the stars. I know that they are not really
stars but that they are angels that are guarding us.

I give thanks to you because of the things that you give us
without our asking.

Thank you for giving me this precious gift . . . that is life.
Amen.

*Tania Castrejón DeOrlow*
*Saint Ambrose School, Houston, TX*

## A Camper's Thanks

Thank you, God, for tall pine trees,
the bee's buzz, and a cool breeze;
for a walking stick to pass the miles away,
for the enjoyment of each day;
for brown rustic trails, for lobster tails,
for sweet strawberries, wild raspberries too,
apple pie, and campfire stew;
for dark caves, and salty waves,
for memories old and new, for the damp dew,
for the red rose, for the grass that tickles your toes,
for a sunny sky so blue.
But most of all, God, I thank you for you!

*Andrew Forecki*
*Saint Mary School, Hales Corner, WI*

★★★

Dear God,
I just want to say "hi!"
I want to say that I'm having a good day.
Thanks to you,
    I have had a breakfast,
    I have had a lunch,
    I have had a dinner.
Thank you, dear God,
    For I have a nice house,
    I have lots of friends,
    And my life is pretty good.
Thanks, God,
    For water to drink,
    For big maple trees,
    For dogs that bark,
    For juicy oranges,
    And small green grapes.
But thanks most of all
    for a miraculous thing called life.
Amen.

*Tracy M. Jarvis*
*Mount Saint Joseph Academy, Buffalo, NY*


★★★

Dear God,
Thank you for my hands and feet.
Thank you for the food we eat.
Thank you for the flowers that grow.
Thank you for the pure white snow.
Thank you for my family.
Thank you, God, for loving me!
Amen.

*Emily Pilgrim*
*Precious Blood Parish, Dayton, OH*

Jesus, thank you for all the people of the world.
You give us people to love,
> but sometimes we do not love all people.

Thank you, God, for loving us anyway.

Jesus, thank you for all our wonderful talents.
You give us all wonderful talents,
> but sometimes we do not use our talents to serve you.

Thank you, God, for loving us anyway.

Jesus, thank you for giving us free will.
You give us many choices,
> but sometimes we do not make good choices.

Thank you, God, for loving us anyway.

Jesus, thank you for showing your love to us.
You show your love to us in many ways,
> but sometimes we do not take the time to notice.

Thank you, God, for loving us anyway.

Jesus, thank you for giving us life.
You give us our life and the lives of others,
> but sometimes we take our life and the lives of others.

Thank you, God, for loving us anyway.

Jesus, thank you for giving us your life.
You made the ultimate sacrifice for us,
> but sometimes we still disrespect you.

Thank you, God, for loving us anyway.

*Karen*
*Cathedral Carmel School, Lafayette, LA*

God in heaven, up above,
Thank you for the ones I love.

For my parents, who love and care;
When I need help, they're always there.

For my brothers, who like to tease,
But will help me if I say please.

For my grandparents, who tell me about the past;
I hope these memories will always last.

For aunts, uncles, and cousins, too,
And all the fun things that we do.

I see your love every day.
I try to spread it in every way.

*Sarah*
*Holy Cross Catholic Community, West Fargo, ND*


Thanks for all the homework due tomorrow.
Thanks for siblings that are always asking "why?"
Thanks for the toy I couldn't get yesterday.
And thanks for the presents my dog and cat leave me.

Yes, let us be thankful.
Be thankful for the chance to go to school and learn.
Be thankful for the toys we have and the siblings we share
        them with.
And let's be thankful for that cat or dog that will love us to
        the end.
We need to be more thankful.

*E. A. K.*
*FACES Middle School, Fond du Lac, WI*

When I look out the window, what do I see?
I see the wonderful world God created for me:
the sky, the trees, the plants all around,
wildlife and nature hiding, and waiting to be found.

People in cars and walking on streets—
thank you, God, for all the people I meet.
You have blessed me with loving friends and family;
they seem to bring out the best in me.

Thank you, God, for all you have given me.
Please help me to be all I can be.

*Bryan Scheffel*
*Sacred Heart School, Fairfield, OH*

Thank you for my very life and for the air I breathe.
Thank you for the birds that fly and for the fishes in the sea.
Thank you for my family, who have helped me a whole lot,
even for my little brother, who can sometimes be a pain.
Thank you for the moon, the stars, the sky, the clouds, the
        rain.
Thank you for the food I eat and the drinks I drink,
and thank you very much for the things I think.
Thank you for my teachers who have taught me a whole lot.
Thank you for my friends who are there when some are not.
Thank you for these things and more.
But thank you most of all for your love and for my life—
Your greatest gifts of all. Amen.

*Anika J. Guldstrand*
*American Martyrs School, Manhattan Beach, CA*

Thank you, God, for the life you bring me. You created me the way you thought would be nice, and I came out adorable. You, God, are the light of my life because you are always listening. When I'm in trouble, you understand. If I'm having a problem, you care.

God, you love me with all your soul, and I love you with all my soul.

*Elizabeth Marie Raycroft*
*Northeastern Catholic Junior High, Rochester, NY*

Dear God,
I want to give you all my thanks; a special thanks for putting me here on earth and making me who I am. I give you the greatest gratitude for helping me through times of pain and sorrow. Thank you for blessing me with such a powerful conscience that tells me right from wrong. I thank you for giving us your only Son so that we may be saved and have eternal life. God, I ask you to continue helping and supporting me while I struggle to climb the long path to heaven.

*Ryan Kelley*
*Saint Patrick School, Stoneham, MA*

Dear God,
Thank you for everything that I have in my life, including my loving parents and my baby brother. I know I've made mistakes at times, but I will try hard to do my best. Thank you for your forgiveness, and help me to work harder. Please help me to become a more responsible person, and help me to deal with the problems of growing up. Amen.

*Devan Pelon*
*Saint Martha Parish, Okemos, MI*

Dear God,
Sometimes I believe I forget to thank you. You have given me so many great things, and I think I sometimes take advantage of that. So now I want to thank you for my family, friends, and the food I have. I would also like to pray for those who are less fortunate than I am—those who haven't been blessed with the many things I have. I ask you to help so that I will have the courage to reach out to the outcasts that are too often ridiculed. I try to be friends with everyone, but it is not always easy. God, thank you for everything. Amen.

*Rachel E. Cox*
*Our Lady of Hope/Saint Luke School, Baltimore, MD*

Thank you, God . . .
for our parents that help us grow in God's love, working their
	hardest to make sure we receive an education.
for our teachers that teach us responsibility and challenge us
	to do our best.
for the knowledge you give to people to find ways to cure
	diseases.
for the stars that shine so bright to help us see ourselves
	through the dark.
for peacemakers all over the world that make peace among
	people.
for the animals you have given us to observe.
for nature and plants that make food for the animals and
	for us.
for miracles that make wonderful things to help us.
for our emotions that allow us to feel different things.
I especially thank you for myself, and for the chance to
	imagine these things.

*Monique Nuñéz*
*Saint Theresa School, Phoenix, AZ*

God, I thank you for lots of things in my life—my parents, my brother, my sister, my nephew, and my pets. Thank you for my house and for my room.

Most of all, God, I thank you for giving me life. I may not have everything in the world, but I am happy to be me. You take care of me in good times and in bad times. You will be my friend forever, even if I don't have any friends on earth. For this I am grateful. Amen.

*Ann W.*
*Saint Josaphat School, Cheektowaga, NY*

God,
We thank you for our life,
    even if we sometimes struggle in it.
We thank you for our family,
    even if we are sometimes angry with them.
We thank you for all that you give us,
    even when we don't say it.

*Patrick R. Stevenson*
*American Martyrs School, Manhattan Beach, CA*

Oh, God, we are eternally thankful for the life you have given us and for the second chances you give us every day. We are thankful for the love you have shown us and for your everlasting guidance. You have given us the joys of life, friends, and family. You have given us your only Son in order to save our lives. Through him you opened to us the gates of heaven and eternal life. We thank you for your guidance during the rough times and for showing us the light of your ways. Amen.

*M. T.*
*Saint Cyprian School, Sunnyvale, CA*

Dear God,
You above all things and people come first in my life. Sometimes I suffer, but no one has ever suffered as you did to save us. I thank you for the parents you gave me. I thank you for the relatives who are always there for me. I thank you for watching over my family when things happen unexpectedly. I can't thank you enough. I thank you most for creating me, so that I can learn about you and about the wonders of the world. Amen.

*Edward J. Foster IV*
*Saint John Vianney School, Saint Pete Beach, FL*

God,
Help me to celebrate the positives in today's society, and not to lose myself in the negatives. You have given us so much for which to be thankful.
- Thank you for nature and all its beauty, especially in an age when sin defaces our lives.
- Thank you for simplicity in a world of complexity.
- Thank you for love, the one force that sees no barriers— racial, ethnic, religious, or otherwise.
- Thank you for trust, for the bonds it forms do not easily crumble.
- Thank you for *thank you,* the two most powerful words ever spoken.
- God, I praise and thank you for all the positives in my life, for they are too numerous to be listed here.

   Help to keep me from worrying about the negatives in my life, and let me reach inward to touch the child within me and within all of us. A child has no fear, a child has only positives. Help me to focus on the positives in my life, because the more I focus, the more there will be. Amen.

*Kevin Collins*
*Saint Robert School, Shorewood, WI*

Dear God,
I know I don't thank you enough for all you have given me: my family, friends, health, and more. Sometimes it is easy to get wrapped up in everyday life. And sometimes I forget to pray as much as I would like to. I will try harder to remember.

It gets pretty aggravating being in sixth grade and being a sister between two brothers. Please help me to be more tolerant of my family and teachers—and especially of my brothers.

I would like to pray for all the sick people, especially the ones with no one to pray for them. Also, I would like to pray for the homeless people. Please look down on them and help them. Amen.

*Sarah Hietschold*
*Cathedral of Saint Raymond Parish, Joliet, IL*

God Almighty,
I praise you for your goodness
    and for this world you have given us.
I praise you for the moon and sun.
I praise you for beaches and for starlight,
    for breezes to blow the spray of the sea into our face.
I praise you for all that you have given us,
    and most of all, for the gift
    of your Son.

*Stephanie Guertin*
*Saint John Neumann Parish, Knoxville, TN*

God,
We sometimes forget that we are more fortunate than others. We have a warm home while others sleep in cardboard boxes. We have full stomachs and throw away leftovers while some go to sleep only dreaming of food. While we are healthily jogging down the street, we pass by those who are ill and dying, lying on our benches. And most important, we have loving families who bring happy memories, while those who are orphaned search for the reason why they were left alone. So, God, give us the strength and compassion to put comfort into the life of those who are less fortunate.

*Steven Asbaghi*
*American Martyrs School, Manhattan Beach, CA*

Dear God,
I thank you for everything in my life—for my joy, my happiness, and, at times, my pain. I thank you for my family that I love so much, and I thank you that my family is healthy, and that my stepmother's father will enjoy his life in heaven. I thank you also for my animals that are there when I need someone to talk to. I thank you for the earth that is so beautiful when it blooms.
  I THANK YOU SO MUCH!
  Last, I thank you for the years at my real home. I loved that house so much. Thank you for the memories of my real family. But most of all, God, I thank you for making me.

*Ashley Grinnell*
*Saint John of Rochester School, Fairport, NY*

I thank you for loving me and showing me you're there.
Thank you, God, for blessing me with people who care.
I know you love us, your creations you have made,
For you sent your only Son, a true price for us you have paid.

It's hard growing up these days, I know you understand.
I'm so glad you're there, lending a helping hand.
It sometimes feels like we're all alone in the world, without
     even a friend.
But comfort that warms my soul, you send.

This is why every night I pray,
And from the bottom of my heart, I can truly say,
I love you, Lord Jesus Christ,
My savior and friend.

*Aleshia Bonis*
*Saint Michael Parish, Beaver Dam, WI*


God, thank you for being the one I could turn to in my time
     of need.
You have been and will always be there for me.
     When I was alone, talking to you kept me company.
     When I was sad, thinking of you made me happy.
     When I was grieving, praying to you made my pain go
          away.
     When I was feeling hopeless, having faith in you made
          me hopeful.
God, the only way I can thank you is by offering my life to you.
Please except my only gift, for it is time I did something for
     you.
Amen.

*Erin O'Brien*
*Sacred Heart School, Bayside, NY*

God,
Thank you for love,
    in which we realize the needs of others.
Thank you for our own little world,
    in which we all wander.
Thank you for our dreams,
    in which we all believe that they will come true
        someday.
Thank you for endings,
    in which we all can find new beginnings.
Thank you for death,
    in which we all realize the importance of life.
And most important, thank you for your Son,
    who gave his life for ours.
Amen.

*Luke Behnke*
*Saint Roman School, Milwaukee, WI*


Dear God,
I am thankful for the fish in the sea,
I am thankful for being me.
I am thankful for playing football with my friends,
I am thankful for the fun that never ends.
I am thankful for fishing off a pier,
I am thankful for hunting deer.
I am thankful for the birds in the sky,
I will be thankful till the day that I die.
Amen.

*Andy Konitzer*
*Saint John the Baptist School, Howard, WI*

Thank you, God, for making me, me. I love myself, and that is important to me. I have my own personality, my own image, and my own way of thinking. I pray that all people would be themselves whether they are around family, friends, classmates, teachers, or any other person. All people that you have made have their own great and distinct personality, and there is no reason not to show the real you. Please help all people to be themselves and to truly love themselves. Amen.

*April Marie Kick*
*Saint Thomas More School, Omaha, NE*

You made the sky a brilliant blue.
You made the sun and the ocean, too.
And so I thank you, God.

You created the moon and stars above.
You created everyone I love.
And so I thank you, God.

You created the forests, the deserts of sand.
We are all safe in the palm of your hand.
And so I thank you, God.

The robins sing, the doves coo.
All of this is because of you.
And so I thank you, God.

You made all the creatures on the earth.
You gave them life; you helped them birth.
And so I thank you, God.

Thank you, God, for all your love.
I know you're watching from heaven above.
And so I thank you, God.
Amen.

*Katie Carder*
*Saint Michael School, Albion, NE*

★★★

Thank you, God,
 for apples and attitudes of love,
  bananas and bears,
  cute, cuddly cats and carrots,
  dynamite dads,
  elephants and chicken eggs,
  frogs and fun times and fish,
  giraffes,
  happy times and neat hats,
 for igloos and icicles and ice cream,
  jaguars and janitors,
  kangaroos and kites,
  lightbulbs,
  mothers and *not* for math,
  nice people and neat papers,
  ostriches and good omens,
 for adorable platypuses and perfume,
  quiet time and queens,
  righteousness and rings,
  summertime and strawberries,
  toddlers and turtles,
  umbrellas and utter laughter,
 for very nice views,
 for the word *why*
 for xylophones and Francis Xavier,
  yaks, yams, and yodelers,
 for zany zoos.
  I thank you.

*Susan Marie Bronk*
*Saint Stanislaus School, Winona, MN*

God, thank you:
For all living things,
For all people on earth,
For all animals on earth,
For all suns and moons,
For all nights and days,
For all time,
For all creation.
Thank you, God.

*John L. Holm*
*Good Shepherd Parish, Huntsville, AL*

# Part Three

# Prayers for Growing Up

going to be ~~pures~~, but I ~~~~
are there next to me. I am ~~~~
that I am me Please h j        Dear ~~Go~~
me thm~~~~                      I am thankf~~~~
~~chai~~                 loving family I
God, please he]      wonderful friends
homework bear   the person I am.
at times    as   lucky as I am.
please I   thankful for the pe~~~~
Amen    Always love you. Amen.
          be with me.

~~~~usses you. Grant
~~~~od the Father, God the Son
~~~~od the Holy Spirit
                    ✠ Amen ✠

~~Y~~ear God,

Thank you ~~frmily~~ for my family
and my   athletic ability.
And if, Oh God, you could make me taller,
I know in my heart I would still be
~~I was~~ ~~servant~~. the person you
          me.

          ~~~~ and eat,
          ~~~~ and com~~~~

Dear God and Jesus, too,
Sometimes I don't understand your ways of showing me
things, such as those valuable life lessons that I get from
Mom. However, I guess they'll be good for me when I grow
up and have to deal with bosses and coworkers and such.
I wonder what I'll be when I grow up. Something for you,
whatever it is. I hope that I don't forget that as I get older.

Now, as I'm growing up, I'm worrying more and more
about forgetting things like dolls, stuffed animals, and science
fiction and fantasy books. Please, God, help me hold on to
the good things of life as I grow and mature. With your help
and following your will, I ought to give it a shot. Maybe
that's what life's about. I love you, God. I pray that others
may come to know and love you the way that I try to. Amen.

*Anna*
*Saint James Parish, Cazenovia, NY*

**Second Best**

Is that all I am?
Next to first.
I'm not perfect.
Never going to be the best.
I'm not ranked "high importance."
What has to be done to live as equals?
God has no second best.
In God's eyes we're perfect.
God doesn't give labels.
We're all number one.

*Amy Mueller*
*Saint Mary Parish, Geneva, MN*

Most loving God,
Guide me through all the roads that I take in life.
Be my light through the darkness,
    my direction when I am lost,
    my courage when I am afraid,
    my comfort when I am feeling down,
    and my strength when I struggle.
For you are the one, God, each and every day,
Watching over me as I work and play.

*Brendan Lill*
*Saint Pius X School, Loudonville, NY*

Lunch begins.
The kids pile in.
Laughter erupts from their mouths.
They save spots for their friends.
They always push me to the end.
Yes, you know me.
    I am the girl you call fat.
    I am the boy that never talks.
    You call me four eyes.
I'm the weird one.
I'm the one
    always ignored,
    always pushed aside.
All I want is to talk to you,
    to be accepted into the group.
And for once could I sit by you?
    That would be a dream come true.
If just one time I wasn't alone.
If just once I was cool enough
    to receive an invitation to lunch.

*Missy L. Dondlinger*
*Saint Thomas Aquinas School, Wichita, KS*

God in heaven, guide me this school year in many ways. Help me not to dwell on my mistakes but to learn and improve from them. Lead me in spending my time wisely and efficiently. Help me not to get scared or shaken up when I do not understand something, and always help me to remember that it does not matter what grades we get but how hard we try. Amen.

*Nick Hamilton-Cotter*
*Saint Bartholomew School, Bethesda, MD*

Dear God,
Please help my peers and me as we take another step into our future. Help us to develop new friendships and to keep and treasure the friendships we have acquired. Help us to make the right choices and to learn from our mistakes. Help us to always know how important our families are. And protect us as we grow in our faith and our love for you.

*Frank*
*Saint Pius X School, Loudonville, NY*

![three stars]

Dear Jesus, help me with life's obstacles.
    When I am tempted, let me choose correctly.
    When I am angry, let me try to forgive.
    When I am sad, let me find happiness.
Dear Jesus, help me with my life's choices.

*Michael Baldwin*
*Our Lady of the Rosary School, Greenville, SC*

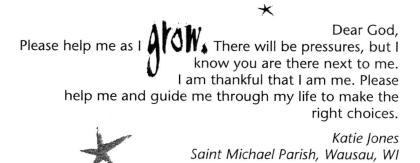

Dear God,
Please help me as I **grow.** There will be pressures, but I know you are there next to me. I am thankful that I am me. Please help me and guide me through my life to make the right choices.

*Katie Jones*
*Saint Michael Parish, Wausau, WI*

God, please help me with my homework, because it can be **HARD** at times. And **SO CAN LIFE,** so please help me with life, too. Amen.

*Derek*
*Saint Liborius Parish, Saint Libory, IL*

Dear God,
As I stare out my bedroom window looking into the dark night, I wonder who I am and why I am here. Why was I made, and again, who am I really? Will you share with me the answer? Am I the only one who wonders? I wonder who you are. I believe you are there in my heart, but my brain goes on into deeper understanding and harder questions. Sometimes I forget who I am, and then I snap back to reality, confused as ever. Please give me the strength and courage to go on and learn what you're trying to teach me.

*Christina Chin*
*Our Lady of Mercy School, Rochester, NY*

★★★

Dear God:
Let my life be filled with joy,
And let me find a decent boy.
Let my spirit be real high,
So high I can fly.
Please don't let me be down, it's the pits,
And I really want to get rid of my zits.
Thank you, God, for my mom.
Please, God, let me find a date to the prom.
Thank you, God, for my dad;
He seems to think he's really rad.

God, I know this is a lot to ask,
But I know you can do any task.
Please, God, keep me safe.

*Stephanie Huften*
*Saint John the Evangelist School, Severna Park, MD*


★★★

Dear God,
Sometimes we ask you to help us in a game. We ask that we don't miss a serve or a free shot, or hit the ball into the tennis net. But we should say "thank you," for being able to play a sport. Sports aren't everything. We can't make it to heaven by playing sports. We know that we can get a step higher by praying and proving that you're more important to us. So instead of missing Mass because of a soccer game on Sunday, maybe we can skip the game or go to Mass on Saturday night.

*Danielle Bremer*
*Saint Mary Cathedral School, Cape Girardeau, MO*

Dear God,
Why am I not growing? I am the shortest kid on the basketball team and in the school. I am eating and exercising correctly, but my weight gain is minimal. If I were bigger, I would be stronger, and maybe I would be a better athlete. Being small does not affect my lifestyle. I know that I will grow at some time or the other, but the sooner the better.

*Parker Turczyn*
*Shrine Academy, Royal Oak, MI*

Oh, dear God, please help me to better understand other people's feelings before I say or do anything to hurt them. Please help me to try to understand how I would feel if I were in their shoes. I know that with your help, if we all learned to treat people how we want to be treated, there would be more peace in the world.

*Shannon Sanacora*
*Saint Michael School, Netcong, NJ*

I want to be better . . .
    if only I could have the perfect hairstyle
    if only I could have the perfect smile
    if only I could have designer clothes
    if only I could be the smartest
    if only I could be the nicest
    if only I could have all the riches I desire
But I don't need all these things, because I'm God's child and number one in God's heart.

*Dustin Meredith Almon*
*Saint John the Evangelist School, Severna Park, MD*

Dear God,
Right now I am going through a lot of changes. Soon I will be graduating from grade school. I'm not sure I'm ready for the changes coming, or prepared for them. Graduation is a frightening thought. But in a way, I'm also looking forward to my next four years of high school. Please help me find the answers that I seek, and give me courage to handle any situation I face. Amen.

*Ursula Winters*
*Our Lady of Victory School, Floral Park, NY*

Dear God,
Thank you for my family
and for my athletic ability.
And if, oh God,
you could make me

# taller,

I know in my heart
I would still be
the person you made me.

*Jim Mula*
*Saints Anthony and Joseph Parish, Herkimer, NY*

When I wake, I dress and eat.

During class, I learn and compete.

After school, study is a must.

In all my endeavors, **in Jesus Christ I trust.**

*Tim Kopec*
*Saint Clare of Montefalco School, Grosse Pointe Park, MI*

Dear God,
I would like to ask you a question about peer pressure. I am always wondering if I will have a lot of peer pressure when I go into high school. I don't have much right now, and for that I thank you. But I would like you to give me the wisdom to make good choices so that I will do the right things. Please don't let power, possessions, or pleasure run my life.

In high school I hope I fit in, but not because I have clothes that everyone likes or something that everyone thinks is cool. I hope I never do drugs, so please help me to say no at the right time and always to say yes to you.

*Jared Matthews*
*Saint Mary Regional School, West Plains, MO*

Dear God,
Being a preteen is a lot of pressure. I mean, it is very difficult when you are getting more involved in your social life, and at my age that tends to mean the world to a lot of children. I try not to lose faith in you or forget about you, because you are the right path.

One of my favorite Proverbs is 16:33: *You may make your plans, but God directs your actions.* Most of the time I feel that this is true, because I believe that in everything I do, you will be right behind me, giving me a little push onto the right path.

Many children out there, dear God, want to follow in your footsteps, but it is really hard, especially if they fall into temptation. Sometimes I feel as if you are not there. But I know you are, because you love all your children, and you will always be there to help us, guide us on the path of righteousness, and protect us. In the name of Jesus I pray. Amen!

*Corinne Concepción*
*De La Salle Academy, New York, NY*

God, please help me and others who are having trouble.
Guide me through right and wrong.
I need to know when I should say no,
or if I should do something, or if I shouldn't.
Sometimes I get caught up in goofing around
and I can't stop.
Will you help me if I am going overboard
or doing something wrong?
Other kids are egging houses or doing worse.
Will you help them, too?

*Vince Pivirotto*
*Our Lady of Angels Parish, Burlingame, CA*


Dear God,
Help me in everything I do.
Let me be healthy,
    and let me be safe in your hands.

Guide me, O God.
Please be with me.
Let me share peace with others.
Help me to be a patient person,
    to be nice and kind to everyone around me.

I ask you, God,
    to help me grow up to do your work.
Bless me, O God.
Be with me as I grow.
Amen.

*Kathy Vang*
*Saint Jerome School, Maplewood, MN*

Help me today
as I go to school.
Help to remember
the Golden Rule.

Thanks for making
it possible, God,
to get to school safely
by getting on board.

I know you're with me
every day.
Thank you for helping
in every way.

Gentle the hands,
the minds of my peers,
so no one gets hurt
or sheds any tears.

Help me to teach.
Help me to grow.
Help me to remember
all that I know.

Make me
an example, please.
Hold my tongue,
so that I don't tease.

Help me always,
and I'll thank you
every single day
for all that you do.

*Star Udell Clark*
*Villa Maria School, Erie, PA*

O God,
Please guide me through my teen years, and help me to make the right choices. Watch over me in good and bad times. Please help me in high school to be a good leader and a good person. Help me to handle all the pressures of life, and also help me to love other people as much as I love myself. Guide me through life so I may respect my elders, peers, and younger ones. Keep me healthy and safe. In Jesus Christ our Lord's name, amen.

*J. Fuentes*
*Saint Margaret Mary School, Lomita, CA*

God, I need to talk to you. I am so confused about my life and about what I am supposed to do. I mean, what is my part in life here? My mom and dad make me feel like I'm not wanted. Maybe that's just not it, but it just feels like that. It seems to me as if I were in a dark room all alone by myself with no one to talk to. I don't know anything about my life. I don't know about my past; I don't know what to do anymore. Anyway, what I'm asking for is lots of strength and love.

*Name Withheld*
*Church of the Risen Christ Parish, Denver, CO*

Dear God,
Hey, what's up up there? I know I am not very good, but please help me with my grades and my relationships with others. And if you could help me to be on time more often, I would really appreciate it. Love,

*Joey Overby*
*Saint Elizabeth Ann Seton Parish, Fort Collins, CO*

Dear God,
Guide me through this rough time in my life. It is hard sometimes to act as a good Catholic should. I have temptations in my life, and sometimes it's hard to ignore them. I want you to know that I try my best. I have so much going on in my life—like starting high school, getting good grades, being the best friend I can, and compromising with my parents— it's very confusing. Sometimes my parents don't understand me, and it's very frustrating. I know I can talk to you anytime and you'll be there. Thank you!

*Erin Young*
*Saint John School, Westminster, MD*

O my God, give me the strength I need to face
the challenges of life as I grow. Help me to accept and
understand what is going on around me in my times of need.
Help me, too, as I face the real world.

*James Powers*
*American Martyrs School, Manhattan Beach, CA*

**Wisdom Bringer,** you help me through my tests.

(Except sometimes I think you forget about math and

Spanish tests!)

You help me to choose right instead of wrong.

You help me to choose fun instead of being bad.

Thank you.

*David D. Miller*
*Saint Stanislaus School, Winona, MN*

Dear God,
This is a time in my life when I need you most. I'm growing up, and I'm going to face tough decisions. Help me to make the right decisions; they might change the rest of my life. My life is like a puzzle; there are pieces that don't fit and even some pieces that are missing. As you can see, my puzzle isn't finished, and I need your help and guidance to finish it. I truly appreciate you in my life. Thank you for the many blessings.

*Cara Jade Riederer*
*FACES Middle School, Fond du Lac, WI*

Dear God,
Help me to be a good friend to my friends. I am going into high school soon and will probably need them most then. In order to keep my friends, I'll need your help. Help me to be patient and kind to them and to stand by them when no one else does. Please help me be a good friend. Amen.

*Delece Smith-Barrow*
*Saint Ann Academy, Washington, DC*

O God, help me with the things I need help with. I know I am not perfect, but I try to do your work and follow you. I know some of my problems are small to some people, but they are big problems to me. I need your guidance in solving them. Help me in my daily struggle to be like you. Help me to put others first and myself last.

*Megan A. Chlarson*
*Saint Thomas the Apostle School, Phoenix, AZ*

Dear God,

    I want to wear the latest fashions, the coolest jewelry.

    I want to have the latest hairdo, the most-wanted shoes.

    I want the newest CDs and the best grades.

Dear God, I know these things may seem important right now, but they're not.

    I want my parents to be proud of me and to be reasonable.

    I want the whole world to love me and understand me.

    I want to have lots of friends and to be true to my friends.

Dear God, I know these are the important things. I know you won't just hand these over to me, but help me to work toward them myself.

*Name Withheld*
*Jackson Catholic Middle School, Jackson, MI*

Dear God,

Help me throughout the years of my life. Help me overcome any obstacle that stands in my way. When I'm in doubt and feeling alone, give me hope and be my friend. When I'm in a fix, talk me through it. When I am so mad that I feel like I want to hurt whomever is in my way, calm me so I can cool off and feel better. And when I am very depressed to the point of suicide, or when I want to give up on everything, cheer me up and make me laugh.

    God, I know you will always look over me and help me throughout all the years of my life. Amen.

*Joe Palmer*
*Saint Peter School, Huber Heights, OH*

You say we should love
one another, but it's hard
when other people don't
love you. Most people just
look at what's on the
**outside** instead of what's on the **inside.**
Please help people see
past what's on the outside.

*Scott Jaworski*
*Saint Raphael the Archangel Parish, Oshkosh, WI*

Loving God,

You know ***everything*** about me and ***everything*** that

will happen to me, sad and joyful. Please help me to find

a vocation that uses my talents and pleases you. Amen.

*Sally Oelschlegel*
*Incarnate Word Academy, Corpus Christi, TX*

Gracious God,
I try to make the right decisions,
    but sometimes I am misguided.
I try to be nice to other people,
    but sometimes I lose my patience.
Sometimes I lose hope,
    but then I remember that you are with me,
    guiding me, forgiving me, and loving me.
Thank you.
Amen.

*Kimberly DePaul*
*Holy Rosary School, Claymont, DE*

My parents tell me I have the wrong
answer on my homework, and I say
I DON'T CARE.
My coach tells me I'm shooting my
layups wrong, and I say
I DON'T CARE.
My friend gets mad at me and says she
will never be my friend again, and I say
I DON'T CARE
And for all those other times when I say
I DON'T CARE,
I really do.
I really do care.

*Jacquline Barrie*
*Holy Spirit School, Louisville, KY*

God:
Please help all the teenagers to know that they *are* someone.
    Someone who is cared about by others.
    Someone who has the power to resist negativity.
    Someone who can make a difference.
Help them to be strong when their world seems to come
    crashing down around them.
Help them stand up for what is right when everyone else
    believes in what is wrong.
Help them appreciate themselves when they do something
    good.
Help them know that it is okay to make mistakes, because
    they will always be loved by you. Amen.

*Chelsea Garland*
*Saint John the Baptist School, Howard, WI*

God, grant me patience, the will to wait.
Help me to listen, even if the subject is dull.
Don't let me get frustrated, God.
Give me the grace to see it through.
It is hard to go day after day, week after week doing the
    same old things.
I want to listen and to be interested.
Help me, God.
I need it day after day, week after week.

*Caitlin Forst*
*Saint John School, Westminster, MD*

God, please help us as individuals to go our own way and to
do our different activities. We all must realize that what is
right is not always popular and what is popular is not always
right. If we make choices that are influenced by our friends,
we might not have wanted that, or we might have been
happier with the other choice. If you are just trying to fit in,
you probably are not fitting in with what Jesus preached.

*Nick J. Peranteau*
*Saint Vincent de Paul School, Rogers, AR*

Dear God,
Oh Lord, my God, forgive me. I ask you to bless me before
this test so that I do my very best. I've studied and studied.
I am prepared, so with your help, I won't be scared. I know
I've sinned, but I ask your forgiveness. Lead me and guide
me to try my hardest and to please you. Amen.

*Jamie J. Nieto*
*Saint Maria Goretti School, Schiller Park, IL*

Dear God,
Help me with my daily stresses,
    namely homework, peer pressure, and brothers and
        sisters.
Help me to speak what I know,
    but I am a teenager, and do not know anything.
Things become confusing,
    (and school becomes annoying.)
Help me keep my cool,
    accept failure,
    and make my way
    through this day.
Tomorrow I'll worry about the next.

*John Lorenz*
*Saint Agnes School, Fort Wright, KY*

Oh God, I saw a butterfly today.
I saw how perfectly it was designed,
and, God, how it goes through
the stages of its life.

I ask you to help me
through the stages of my life,
to go through it caringly, lovingly,
and most of all, with your help.

For with your help I can go
through the stages of my life;
I can do what you would
like me to do. Amen.

*Anne Zagrodnik*
*Saint Mary on the Hill School, Augusta, GA*

As I journey through my growing years, help me to stay focused and not to go astray. Please, dear Jesus, give me the strength to do your will and not mine. When temptations surround me, give me the courage to walk away. Keep me safe from all evils of the world. Send your angels to guide and protect me.

When you became a human being, you dealt with life's pressures and overcame all of them by turning to God in heaven. Help me to follow your example and become Spirit-guided in my thoughts, words, and actions. Amen.

*Ashley Quintanilla*
*Seton Catholic Junior High School, Houston, TX*

God, I thank you for everything I have. Without you I would have nothing; you give me strength to go on. In the good times and the bad times, you are with me no matter what. I don't know what I would do without your guidance and love.

Give me courage to say no to things that might turn me away from doing your will and to things that could affect my life forever. Give me wisdom to know right from wrong and to always make good choices throughout my life. Amen!

*Katherine Cerami*
*Our Mother of Sorrows School, Rochester, NY*

O God,

Help me with life.

Help me to choose what is good.

*Show me the way.*

Jorge M. Lastra
Saint Joseph School, Tampa, FL

Dear God,
Help me to get through junior high successfully.
Help me to realize that I will not always have the same friends
and I should be nice to everyone.
Help me to not give in to peer pressure and to not always do
the "cool thing,"
Help me to serve you and others as Jesus would have done.
I know junior high is a hard time, but it is easier when I know
you are there for me forever. Amen.

*Margaret Ann Nichols*
*Holy Spirit School, Louisville, KY*

Dear God,
I've always wondered what you have in store for me. I know
it's not my job to pry, but I would feel better if I knew which
direction I am heading in. As a teenager, my emotions are
heightened and my soul is confused. I'm looking to you to
define what plans you have in store for me. Thanks for the
help you've already given me.

*Rebecca Noonan*
*Saint Roman School, Milwaukee, WI*

Dear God,
Attitude is everything. So today help me find interest in something. I know that motivation is the key to success. So throughout the day, could you help me get motivated? Attitude is everything—could you help with mine? Amen.

*Scott Ball*
*Jackson Catholic Middle School, Jackson, MI*

Dear God,
It's very hard for me to find my group, especially when I need friends most. God, I know I can always talk to you, but I need someone to talk to, someone who won't blab around what I have to say. I need a friend that I can hang out with and that I can pour out all my problems and ideas to. I need someone who's just there to hold my hand. God, help me find more special friends.

*Theresa Parsons*
*Regina Elementary School, Iowa City, IA*

![stars](three stars)

Dear Jesus,
I feel lousy today. Rainy days always make me tired. I couldn't find my shoes anywhere so I had to wear my old ones that don't fit. I looked everywhere for my shoes. Please help me find them!

   Also, thank you for the great weekend you gave me. I had lots of fun on my bike ride. I hope my day gets better when the soccer game starts. I know that whatever you have in store for me will be the best.

*Andy*
*Holy Family Junior High School, Elmira, NY*

God, sometimes I am frustrated,
    but you are there for me.
Sometimes I lie,
    but you always seem to understand.
Sometimes I don't think I need you,
    but you never turn your back.
Sometimes I quit,
    but you believe I can accomplish my goals in life
    and spread the Good News—
about you.
Amen.

*David James Allen*
*Saint John the Evangelist School, Severna Park, MD*

Dear God,
Sometimes I feel so confused about things. Help me to realize
    that you are always with me, no matter how complicated
    life seems.
Sometimes I feel lonely. Help me to know that you are by my
    side.
Sometimes I forget to follow your rule. Please forgive me.
    Help me to know and make the right choices. I will try to
    do what you would do in any situation. Help me to trust
    and love you.
Amen.

*Lisa Messineo*
*Saint Charles Borromeo School, Syracuse, NY*

Dear God,
Please guide me through the long and hard school days.
Keep me awake during the boring classes. Help me through
the unpleasant lunches. Remind me to turn in my math
assignment. Make sure I run hard at basketball practice.
Most of all please stand by me as the world continues to go
on. You are—and always will be—my best friend!

*Brandi Burkhart*
*Saint Mary Parish, Garden City, KS*

God,
Even though I'm not the best at sports, or the best student,
you still love me and take care of me. I might not be the
best-dressed or the best-looking, but you created me in your
image, and you love me. I might not be popular, but I try my
best to be a good, caring, helpful Christian. And you love me
just the way I am. That's all that matters. Amen.

*Christine Mueller*
*Saint John the Evangelist School, Severna Park, MD*

Dear God,
All the wonders of the world are yet to be explored.
Help me to not be scared of what is to come.
Help me to face the dangers and unknowns ahead of me
        with courage and hope.
Give me peace of mind and good judgment.
I need to find my place in the world.

*Ben Howell*
*Saint Robert School, Shorewood, WI*

Today might be the day, or tomorrow, or the day after, but soon the day will come when I will be on my own. Lord Jesus Christ, guide me on my path so that I can learn your ways and learn to be in peace with all. Lead me, teach me your ways, and keep me safe. Forever, I will love you. Amen.

*Hannah C. Snedeker*
*Holy Spirit School, Louisville, KY*

# Friends and Family

the name of the Father, protect.
the name of th
the name of
world. Amen

Father in heaven
    Hear my prayer.
  Keep me in thy loving care.
      Be my guide in all I do.

ld to
red to

r Lord,
me through    bless all those who love me too.
it go by
    AMEN

...d. Plea

help me think not of wha
Want, but what others ne
        Amen

heal ~ to  you; hoping  d, hurt, or
    me  in  anyway
Lord, help me to for
who hurt me in
To this I say

Help
said.

Dear God,
Thank you. You have walked by me every step of the way. I have seen your love shining upon me when you let my mother overcome her cancer. If she were not here, who would pack my lunch? pick me up when I fall? We need her here. I need her love and guidance. You helped her during all the sickness. Please continue to help her, to help her stay strong for the rest of her life. Amen.
A grateful girl,

*Claire LeDuc*
*Highland Catholic School, Saint Paul, MN*

Dear God,
I pray that you will bring my mom closer to our family. And if you do, please let her have a safe trip, whether in a car or in her heart. Just please bring her closer—someway, somehow. Amen.

*Matthew James Gerber*
*Saint Mary Parish, Garden City, KS*

Dear God,
My friend lives thirty miles away, so it's hard for me to see him. And with school it's hard to talk to him. I would like him to move closer, but that isn't going to happen. We had a great friendship until he had to move. Now it's hard to stay in touch with him. He was one of the first friends I made, so it's very important to me to see how he is doing. Take care of him.

*Ben Tassin*
*Shrine Academy, Royal Oak, MI*

Dear God,
I pray that you will help my family get through each day.
Love them as well as teach them to love.
Care for them as well as teach them to care for others.
Watch over them as well as teach them to watch out for
    others.
Keep them safe in this world of harsh realities.
Teach them to love others as if they were their own.
Help them to find goodness in other people, even when it
    isn't very obvious.
I pray that you will give them the strength to get through
    daily obstacles, large and small, and guide them in
    their decisions.
Continue to make it evident that you are here among us.
Amen.

*Rebecca Owings*
*Saint Louis School, Clarksville, MD*

God in heaven, hear my prayer.
I wish to ask a favor.
For my brother—
Please keep him in loving arms,
And help him in all he does.
Please keep an eye on him,
And please make sure he behaves.
For where he is now, he is not happy,
And neither are my mom and I.
This favor is very important to me.
Amen.

*Name Withheld*
*Saint Ann Parish, Bethany Beach, DE*

"Where are you, Grandpa?"
I don't know what to do. Why did Grandpa go?
I know that he is in heaven, but what will he do there?
Will he be an angel, with wings of silk?
Or will he just look down upon us from afar and guide us in
    every decision?
Will he see his parents?
One of my biggest questions is, Will he be happy?
Will we see him in our dreams? I do now, sometimes.
I always pretend that he is here, right beside me through it all.
I miss him.
When I get scared, I just close my eyes and see him smiling
    at me.
I can hear him all the time. He is like a second guardian angel.
It's like a dream.
If something goes wrong, I can just say,
"Wake up. Wake up."

*Catherine M. Linn*
*Saint Robert School, Shorewood, WI*


Dear God,
Bless all teachers so that they may spread your word.
Bless them so that they may continue to touch the lives of
    their students.
Bless the teachers, God, for without teachers our minds
        would never be enriched, our souls would never
        know your word, and our hearts would drift astray.
Bless the teachers that have touched my life, for without
        them I could not write this prayer today.
Bless the teachers, God, today and every day.
Amen.

*Alisandra Betina Carnevale*
*Saint Paul School, Princeton, NJ*

Dear God,
I'm asking for your help. My only grandma is alone. My other grandparents have passed away. Grandma is very lonely. I love her dearly, and she's very close to me. I'm asking you to give her more happiness and to let her proceed on with a healthy, happy, and long life. I would be very grateful for your help. Love always . . .

*Meaghan Hosford*
*Saint Joseph Parish, Croton Falls, NY*

Let me have respect, God, for my classmates and peers. Let me respect everyone's thoughts and words and think about and ponder them. Help me to understand how they are feeling about things in their life. Let my actions always reflect my faith and hope in you. Amen.

*Tanner Holford*
*Saint Pius X School, Loudonville, NY*

Loving God, please help me to obey my parents all the time. I don't always respect them as I know I should. I sometimes believe that I know better than they do. I know this is not true. They have lived so much longer than I have, and they know many more things. Please forgive me for all the times when I have disobeyed and not honored my parents. I truly mean this with all my heart. Amen.

*Josh Rankin*
*Saint Peter School, Huber Heights, OH*

## A Sister's Prayer

Oh, God of all nations, creator of birth,
designer of peace and all that is good.
I thank you for this, you've answered my prayers,
you've sent my sister to love and take care.
She is more beautiful than I pictured, so soft and so fair.
So sweet I imagine she'd taste like a pear.
I love her so much, she's brought joy to my life,
even though she may keep me awake in the night.
Through good times and bad times, this promise I keep:
to always be there to help fulfill and support her greatest
dreams.
Amen.

*Angela Sayner*
*Saint Mary School, Hales Corner, WI*

For homework I was writing a pet peeve speech about little brothers and sisters.

Then I began thinking about how lucky we are to have little brothers and sisters to keep us entertained (even though they can be a pain). So I thank you for keeping the life cycle going.

I sit here looking at our neighbor's backyard, thinking of how a dog used to run around back there and play in the snow and of how I used to play with him. So I ask you, God, please let everyone—from animals to people—have a better life up there than they did down here. And please, also help us with our pollution problem.

*Jacob Thole*
*Roncalli Newman Center Parish, La Crosse, WI*

God has been good to me by giving me loving parents who care for me by feeding me, clothing me, helping with homework, and caring when I'm sick. God has blessed me with sisters, who take me places and help me with homework when my parents can't, and a brother to fight with and play Nintendo.

Thank you, God, for helping me know right from wrong and for parents who teach me about caring for others instead of myself. Help me to be sensitive to people who are less fortunate. Thank you, God, for everything. Help me to be a stronger Christian.

*Aaron Ermis*
*Saint Philip the Apostle Parish, El Campo, TX*

I am staring at my starry ceiling in the dark, thinking, What did I do to be in here? Dishes, homework, and laundry is what I *didn't* do. They put me in here for stupid reasons. Sometimes I wish I was somewhere else. It drives me NUTS, what they say and do. But when I am out of here, I'll realize that they put me in here for my own good. Doing stuff I didn't do before was for my own benefit. When I did my homework, I got better grades. After I did my chores, I was rewarded. Parents aren't that bad. They give me love, help, care, and a shoulder to cry on. Sometimes I don't give that back, but I hope they know that I love them. They're great and awesome.

God, I am grateful for parents. They will always be there for me, and they will always love me. And I will always love them.

*Amy Weatherford*
*Saint Peter School, Huber Heights, OH*

God in heaven,
Help me in my time of need. I'm having so many problems with my mother. Am I going through a phase? I don't think so. Everything she says or does to me bugs me. I don't understand her, and I'm sure she doesn't understand me. It seems like I can't please her. Everything I do is either not to her liking or not to her expectations. I want her to understand me, but I'm very different from her. Sometimes I even think she doesn't want me. Please, God, help me to understand her better. In your name I pray. Amen.

*Danielle Coulanges Isles*
*Seton Catholic Junior High School, Houston, TX*

Dear God,
I know I may fight with my brother, but I still love him. I know I yell at my sister and my parents, but I love them, too. I just get so stressed out that I take out my anger on anybody around me. Please, dear God, help me to control my anger.

*Caitlin Tones*
*Regina Elementary School, Iowa City, IA*

God, I have a special friend I'd like to thank you for,
A friend who cares and loves me, every day much more.
Christ, please bless this special friend I keep inside my heart.
For in my life, she is certainly a truly vital part.
She is such a good friend, almost too good to share.
Of course you must have guessed my friend—
My mom, who's always there.

*D. A. S.*
*Saints Peter and Paul School, Saint Thomas, VI*

God,
You have blessed me with wonderful friends.
You have given me
    shoulders to cry on in sadness,
    faces to laugh with in joy,
    and arms to hug in loneliness.
Thank you, God,
for one of the greatest blessings you have bestowed upon me.
God, help me to be a friend who can
    listen,
    laugh,
    and comfort.
Help me to reciprocate the kindness my friends give to me.
Most important, God, please bless my friends.
The love we share cannot be equaled.

*Sarah Lauren Carmody*
*Saint Rose of Lima School, Haddon Heights, NJ*


God in heaven,
I thank you for the gifts you've given me. I ask that you keep
my parents together. They've been fighting lately, and I don't
want to see what it's like to have two different sets of parents.
I've heard people talking about how they feel because their
parents have split up. Those stories aren't always pleasant.
I ask that you let them see the goodness in their hearts, let
them remember why they're together, what they went
through to get there, and what vows they made. I ask you
for this and for all intentions I hold in my heart. Amen.

*Heather Crystal Sowers*
*Seton Catholic Junior High School, Houston, TX*

Dear Jesus,
Please keep my family safe, especially my great-grandma. She fell, and now she is in the hospital. I know that she is old and probably wants to die, but she has so much to live for. I know that if she died, a part of me would die, too. I know that my family feels the same way. We would miss her funny jokes, playing cards with her, and just plain her. She is one of the nicest people that I know. God, please help her to get well soon, and help her to never give up! Amen.
P.S. I love you.

*Jennifer M. Leonard*
*Saint James School, Denver, CO*

God, bless my family and help us to love and care for one another. Help us to get through hard times. Help us to be grateful for our family and to realize how special we really are. Help us to forgive and to realize that we are not perfect. Watch over us, God, and bless us. Amen.

*Christina Jackson*
*Holy Family Junior High School, Elmira, NY*

Dear God,
I have a baby sister, and she is two months old. As I was sitting with her one day, I began to wonder, What would the world be like without babies? not to have their smiling faces, trusting eyes, little hands and feet? God, I pray that one day the killing will end, and the world will be free of abortion again.

*Sarah Flemings*
*Holy Trinity Parish, Peachtree City, GA*

Dear God,

As I sit at home at my dinner table, I see a lot of loving faces.

> They give me love and support.
> They can make me smile or laugh.
> They're always there for me.
> They love me and trust me.

I am thankful for my family, God, because they make me feel important. I feel as if I'm needed. And they help me with my problems.

*Barry Penegor*
*Saint Martin of Tours School, Franklin, WI*

# Finding a Place in the World

If above the turmoil ..nts, from all saints.
we work tog.
There ...

hape my eyes to see peace in the world. Mold
...s to see good in others, and open my eyes to                    do
...rcy and grace, Amen.                               ...an

...ur father, you make the
...better place. You cleanse
...sin. Please help us +
...l, and sin. You

...lp me love my enemies, treasure my
...me prevent fighting, let me be a Friend
...eed. Let your gentle hand touch
...th peace.

Amen.

A cry from within the womb is forever silenced.
No pink bows, no peewee football.
No first dates, no high school graduations.
No weddings and no grandchildren, all because of one
       choice.
Now there is only the memory that there once was a baby,
A baby who cannot cry, cannot learn, and cannot teach.
A cry from within the womb is forever silenced.

*Kristen Murkowski*
*Jackson Catholic Middle School, Jackson, MI*

God, in a world so full of sadness and chaos, help me.
Though I may be young, teach me to make a difference so
the world that I grow in will become a happier, safer place
for all to live. Amen.

*Ms. Nancy's sixth-grade class*
*Saint Mary Parish, Wayne, MI*

God, I wish to have peace in the world.
    There is too much fighting in this world.
God, I wish to have love in the world.
    There is too much hate in this world.
God, I wish to have justice in the world.
    We need more just people in this world.

*Allen Purvis*
*Saint Michael School, Netcong, NJ*

I dream of a world where bombs are not heard of,
And the way of war is not combat
But compromise.

I dream of a world where knives are used
For cutting up supper,
And not to take lives.

I dream of a world where guns are used
For hunting game,
And not for hunting people.

I dream of a world where people of all colors
Join together in happiness,
And do not envy one another.

I dream of a world where drugs are used
For curing illnesses,
And not for the brainless
Who wish to kill themselves.

*Mitchell Alan Kuhns*
*Holy Name School, Racine, WI*

Dear God,
For those who suffer
and for those who cry on this night,
let there be minutes where they
may experience peace.
Love them, God,
when others cannot.
Hear them, God, when they
cry in pain.

*R. S.*
*FACES Middle School, Fond du Lac, WI*

There are so many things to pray for. Some things are hard to put into words. I would like to pray for our earth, though. It is our only home, and yet we treat it so terribly. I pray that we will all come to our senses before it is too late. We must come to respect the earth and all its beauty. We must stop destroying it and give it time to heal. I pray that God will help us to understand that all life deserves a chance. I pray that God will help us stop the destruction and heal the damage. I hope that God will hear all my prayers, even the ones I have not been able to put into words.

*Meg Kinney*
*Saint Pius X Parish, Indianapolis, IN*

Dear God,

God, help me to love my enemies, treasure my neighbors, and prevent fighting. Let me be a friend to those in need. Let your gentle hand **touch the world with peace.**

Amen.

*Jessica Sue Wise*
*Our Lady of the Lakes School, Waterford, MI*

God,
**SHAPE** my eyes to see peace in the world,
**MOLD** my eyes to see good in others,
and **OPEN** my eyes to your mercy and grace. Amen.

*Virginia J. Jones*
*Saint Ann Academy, Washington, DC*

"Hey, guys, there's a new kid," I said.
"Is it a girl?" they replied.
"No," I mumbled. "We never get those,
but it is a really cool guy."
"He's funny," I said. "And pretty smart.
He's tough, and he never cries."
And when I said he had lived through a wreck,
it really lit up their eyes.
I took them to the edge of the playground,
hoping they wouldn't scare.
They looked at me and said his face was messed up,
and he was stuck in a wheelchair.
My heart was burning as they left,
but my friend, his heart sunk.
"It's okay," he said. "They still need to learn,
God doesn't make junk."
I turned around to look at him,
and saw he wasn't there.
A world with discrimination,
to me, is a world unfair.

*Martin Longhi*
*Saint Thomas Aquinas School, Wichita, KS*

★★★

I had a dream that the world was a baby grand piano.
The music it made was like heaven.
If a key didn't work well with another, it was forgiven.
Every key has a tale to tell.
If you listen well, you can hear the unique sound.
The world is the piano.
We are the keys.

*Amanda E. Vaughn*
*Holy Name School, Racine, WI*

God, I ask you to help those who are less fortunate than I am. All the poor and oppressed people, and especially those who have no one to pray for them, need your help. I pray for those who hurt others, so that they will realize what they are doing to the ones they hurt. Last, I pray that everyone will never forget you and will continue to have faith. Amen.

*Ben Kowalczyk*
*Saint Peter School, Lorain, OH*

Oh God, forgive the *misguided* who squabble over trifles.
Oh God, forgive the *misguided* who rankle one another for
       attention.
Oh God, forgive the *misguided* who make others unhappy for
       joy and pleasure.
Oh God, forgive the *misguided* who doubt you, for they are
       the most blind.
Oh God, forgive the *misguided* who steal, for they are weak in
       spirit.
Oh God, why do we fight among ourselves for petty reasons?
Why must people—innocent people—be targets for the
       *misguided?*
Why can't we understand?
We are brothers, sisters, and family.
We must put our desires behind us and move on.
We must move on.
Oh, mighty God, bringer of night and day, empower us to
       beat the thirst—
The thirst for our own pleasure and for other people's pain.

*Charles Niles Parker*
*Gwynedd-Mercy Academy, Springhouse, PA*

As I walk through the city, I see a homeless man begging for money and food. I think to myself, God, why do you do this to people? I read in the news about people dying of AIDS, and again I think to myself, God, why do you do this to people? One of my friends found out that she has cancer. I think to myself, God, why are you doing this to her? Why do you let people suffer, and why do you let them feel pain? You promised you would never forsake us, but it looks to me like you've neglected them. But God said to me, That is why I put people on the earth like you who care, to comfort and care for them. You are blessed with many gifts and talents, so go ahead and use them to help those in need.

*Alisha O'Brien*
*Saint Pius X School, Tulsa, OK*

O my God,
    there is so much injustice
    in the world today.
I ask for your help
    to be a just person.
I need your guiding hand
    to lead me;
I need your love
    to strengthen me
    and give me courage.
I need to know that
    you are always there
    to lead me.
Help me to become just.
Amen.

*Matt Griffiths*
*Gwynedd-Mercy Academy, Springhouse, PA*

One day on the street, I met a man.
He was ragged and old, but took my hand.
He said he was poor and had no bed,
No roof to cover his head,
Only one pair of rags.
No money to get a haircut, which was in a shag.
His beard was long and needed a trim.
His leg was injured and had an artificial limb.
He said he had no close relations.
All he asked for was a small donation.
I said, You are welcome into my home;
I just cannot leave you alone.
People like you cannot be ignored.
What is your name?
He said, "I am the Lord."

*Ashley Hammen*
*Saint Mary School, Storm Lake, IA*


Loving God,
Thank you for my box of crayons. Knowing you made all
these colors helps me to realize that all people are equal, no
matter what color. I'm sure I've learned to love and respect
people for who they are and what they do. Help me always
to keep a clear and truthful mind of openness and originality.
Amen.

*Kristalena Biafore*
*Holy Rosary School, Claymont, DE*

Dear God,
I know that this is a big world you are taking care of. While we have it so good here, we need to remember those who are suffering, such as the families and children who are starving and all those who are at war in this world. Please watch over those who are poor, homeless, and hungry, including those in our own country. With all of the suffering in the world, I would like to thank you for giving me a loving family, good teachers, and good health. Amen.

*Ben Blakeman*
*Saint Vincent de Paul School, Rogers, AR*

I have a dream—
To be loved for who I am,
And not for my looks or style.

I have a dream
Where there are no secrets,
And where I will be forgiven.

I dream about no whispers or tears,
Only joy and laughter are allowed.
The rich will help the poor,
And the strong will help the weak.

Love is a precious thing
That is rare in today's world,
But in this place that I dream of,
Everyone will possess it,
No matter if in poverty or wealth.
Everyone, everywhere will love.

If everyone dreams as I do,
Maybe my dream shall come true.

*Nicole*
*Holy Name School, Racine, WI*

Soaring birds,
Howling wolves,
Waddling penguins,
The wild forest, ever so calm.
The slithering snake
And the grazing buffalo.
All free,
All happy,
Not a worry in the world,
Except the human race.
Why, God?

*Patrick Copps*
*Saint Robert School, Shorewood, WI*

Dear God,
You know we live in a troubled world, and you know that
when we are too proud to look for you in our life that our
heart and our mind are troubled as well.

Help us, God, to abandon our pride and to seek your
presence in our life. Because in finding you, we find peace.
Then, God, grant us courage to be bearers of your peace
in our homes and to our families, in our schools and to our
friends, in our communities and to our neighbors, in our
world—even to our enemies. You have shown us that one life
can make a difference.

So, God, as we go our separate ways, be our peace, and
let us take your peace, bring your peace, give your peace, be
your peace, see your peace, have your peace, and share your
peace until we meet again. Amen.

*Eighth-grade CCD class*
*Saints Peter and Paul Parish, New Braunfels, TX*

To All Saints, from All Saints:

Rise above the turmoil!

If we work together,

There is nothing we cannot do.

We can **help the poor,** we can **save the sick,**
We can do anything **if we work together.**

*Nicholas Remington Traxler*
*All Saints Parish, Mesa, AZ*

O God, you make the world a better place. You cleanse the
world of sin. Please help us to turn away from evil and sin.
**You are the greatest.** Amen.

*Peter Adams*
*Saint Anne School, Somerset, WI*

Dear God,
Many times the first thing you see in our world today is a
mask of hatred, sorrow, and death. If you look beneath that
mask, however, you will see a bright joy and an everlasting
peace blooming in all our hearts and souls.

I want to ask you, dear God, to help unmask us so that
our best can shine for all to see. Please use your strength to
help remove our coverings, and allow us to show our goodness and faith. I pray for the best to shine forth in all so that
this may be a better world in which to live. Amen!

*Alison K. DeBruyckere*
*Saint Patrick School, Stoneham, MA*

These are the things I pray for:

For the poor, that they find shelter and love wherever they
 may be.
For children, that they will understand and respect their
 parents and friends.
For friends, that they consider their friendship most important.
For parents, whose love is shared with each other and with
 whomever they come in contact with.
For the rich, that they may be giving instead of greedy, and
 that they will do whatever they can with their
 privilege.
For all people of the world, an effort for world peace, and
 relief for the sick and suffering.
I pray for rest for the weary, happiness for the sad, love for the
 forgotten and for outcasts, justice for the persecuted
 and the stereotyped, and a genuine kindness toward
 every man, woman, and child in the world. Amen.

*Rachael Rhoades*
*Saint Joseph School, Wauwatosa, WI*

Dear God,
I often wonder what will be surrounding me in fifty years.
Will there be robots doing work we normally do? Or will we
be living in the ocean and on the moon? Where will the
world be? What will it be like? Overcome with love, peace,
violence, hatred—what? I don't know. No one knows.

Oh God, please guide us to leave this world okay, if not
better, for future generations. Amen.

*Emily Jean Feedar*
*Saint Paul School, Genesee Depot, WI*

God,
To think I am so caught up in all my trials and tribulations of
    being a teenager, and I haven't even seen the big picture.
To think I get upset over such trivial things—a bad-hair day,
    catty fights with my friends, a not-so-great test. And I
    haven't even seen the big picture.
To think I focus on myself so much, having not seen the big
    picture.
The big picture.What is the "big picture"? It is the starving
    people on the streets, political problems, the lush jungle
    in some far-off country, the Olympic medalist reaching
    her dream, the tiny ants marching and building their
    home, beautiful hillsides, a writer making the best-seller
    list.
I am only a small piece of the big picture—
A tiny, itsy-bitsy, minuscule piece of it.
And I get upset over a bad-hair day.

*Sarah Hoffman*
*Saint Robert School, Shorewood, WI*

For peace, love, and prosperity,
    pray to God.
For an end to war, famine, and annihilation,
    pray to God.
For a world without violence,
    pray to God.
For happiness, mercy, and hope,
    pray to God.

*Louis A. DiSarno*
*Our Lady of the Sacred Heart Parish, Lackawanna, NY*

Dear God,

Please help me to take on the responsibilities of trying to make the world a better place. God, I will pray and pray often for peace. I have learned that whenever I have a problem, I can turn it over to God in prayer.

I will respect and care for everything on earth. God, you have made this world such a wonderful and joyous place to be, I want to make sure it stays this way for generations to come.

I hope and pray that I will be able to make a difference. I really feel that discrimination, racism, and hate are a sad part of many lives. I truly want peace on earth, and I will work for it. Amen.

*Candace R. Holmes*
*Saint Ambrose School, Rochester, NY*

God,

I don't understand life. Why is there so much violence, hatred, and agony in this world that I live in? Why are there so many abortions, God? Innocent little babies dying for no reason makes absolutely no sense to me. Why do people drink and drive, God, when they know that they are endangering their own life as well as others' lives? Why do people do drugs, commit suicide, and want to hurt others? It's like the world is going insane. We all desperately need your help, God. Please help us to understand and love, and give us the courage to be able to do what we know is right. But most of all, give us your guidance, God, because we never know when our life will be over. I love you, God. Amen.

*Erin M. Gsell*
*Most Holy Name School, Pittsburgh, PA*

God, please help me deal with the pain,
The way people look at me and think I'm insane.
When I walk with my friend to get something for my mother,
People will say, "Look at those Ricans stealing together."
I need you, God, to help me see
That I'm as good as them with a loving family.
I don't see why the issue is race;
To be a different kind is not a disgrace.
If people are racists, I don't really hate them,
Because I am me, and I'm not ashamed of where I came from.
God, thank you for making me who I am;
I will grow up to be a proud Puerto Rican woman!

*Maria Orabona*
*Saint Stephen School, Pennsauken, NJ*

Humans are superior. Why?
All animals are primitive to us. Why?
Why is this world turned upside down?
Because of us? Them? Who?
Why do we spend our time saving the planet?
I know. We did it. We fix it.
Right? I don't know. How can I?
You know, don't you?
Why don't I?
If we're so superior, why not?
I want to know. Please.
Please help me to see why, how, and who.
Amen.

*Christy McCuen*
*Our Lady of the Rosary School, Greenville, SC*

I see no color, I see no race.
I see nothing ugly, just a beautiful face.
You don't speak my language, but I don't care.
Your inner beauty is what counts,
Not your nose, not your hair.
Give us, oh God, two eyes that see
The innermost beauty in you and in me.
Give us all one song to sing.

He's a tenor, I don't sing.
She can't hear, but let's give it a wing.
We don't know the notes, but it sounds good to me.
Black or white, woman or man,
Together we will make harmony.
Give us, oh God, two ears that hear
The beautiful sounds we find so dear.
Give us all one song to sing.

African or Italian, Chinese or Dutch,
Who cares about race;
It shouldn't matter so much.
Everyone knows the main reason we're here—
To love one another every day of the year.
Give us, oh God, one heart that swells
With such warmth and love that no poem can tell.
Give us all one song to sing!

*Jonathan Umpleby*
*Sacred Heart Parish, Waynesboro, GA*

# Part Six

# Tough Times

to be strong and always look on
...ght side.
...give me the courage
...lties.

Dear Jesus,

...want lots of th...
...Sad times
...pictures ...

Please God, watch over me
whatever I do,
wherever I go,
and whatever I say.
Please guide me "know"
and stick...

Dear Lord,
...with you tell
...hand. You
...need. Help
...Jesus...

...in my life
...times. Fro...
...es.

...ar God,
...en I am sad, hurt, or scared
...look to you; hoping you will
...me in anyway you can...
...help me to forgive
...t me in an...
...I say --

God,
Help me in times of need, when everything seems hopeless and I have no one I can turn to. Be there for me when no one else can be. Be my friend, God, when I am alone and need guidance. Protect me from those who follow the darkness. Show me the way to your light. Inspire me to do the good deeds you have told me to do. For you are my God, and I put my faith in you.

*Douglas J. Beshara*
*Saint Pius X School, Tulsa, OK*

Dear God,
Where are you? How come you are not here for me? In times I need you the most, you seem not to be there. People tell me you'll always be with me. If that's true, why can't I see you or feel your presence? I feel alone. I feel deserted. Give me a sign. I want to know if you're there. Dear God, where are you?

*Heather Ann McKernan*
*Saint Anthony of Padua School, Butler, NJ*

Dear Jesus,
Please help me get through my hard times. I know I don't always do what you want, but I try to be good. I know sometimes I don't turn to you, but I always believe. You are my Savior. So now when I pray to you, please answer, because I need you now more than ever.

*J. N. G.*
*All Saints Parish, Mesa, AZ*

Dear God,
The sky is unclear,
    the path is not lit,
        my soul is a maze of darkness.
My heart is unguided,
    my mind is a blank,
        I don't know the way to your heart.
The directions are wrong,
    the signs aren't direct,
        my world is turned upside down.
The future is so uncertain,
    the past is fading,
        the present is speeding so fast.
The song of confusion stirs in my heart,
    the rhythm controls day and night,
        its music commands my whole life.
God, show me the way to your heart.

*Meghann M. Hiscocks*
*Saint Jude the Apostle School, Westlake Village, CA*

Dear God,
Sometimes I feel like I have no one to talk to. Then I realize that I can always talk to you. You will never talk back to me, you will never interrupt me. You always listen to me, no matter what I have to say. I know that you will never tell my secrets to anyone. Sometimes when I really try to listen, I feel that you are talking to me. And now I know that I will always have someone to talk to and that you will never be too busy to listen to me. Amen.

*Kori Kelly*
*Regina Elementary School, Iowa City, IA*

Dear God,
A very special friend of mine is seriously ill. She needs you to walk beside her through good times and bad times. When I look in those big, bright blue eyes, I see a very strong, courageous, and loving young woman. When I pass her in the halls, I see a vision of you, O God. Just thinking and knowing that one day she will not be here to brighten up my day makes me feel empty inside. God, help me to be strong like her and to always be courageous.

*Crystal*
*Saint Michael Parish, Kalida, OH*

Dear Jesus,

I want lots of things to change in my life—

from the sad times to the lonely times, from the angry times

to the embarrassed times. But please

## let me appreciate life.

*Name Withheld*
*Church of the Risen Christ Parish, Denver, CO*

Dear God,
Help me to be strong
and to always look
on the bright side.
Please give me the

## COURAGE

to overcome difficulties.

*Lindsay D. Martin*
*Saint Theresa School, Phoenix, AZ*

God,
When I feel I can't go on,
   give me strength.
When my insides feel like a raging sea,
   give me peace.
When nothing is going right,
   give me hope.
When I can't decide which path to choose,
   give me guidance.
When nothing seems to have any reason,
   give me understanding.
Help me to believe I am truly never alone in you.

*Ashley Lang*
*Saint John the Evangelist School, Severna Park, MD*

Dear God,
"Why have you forsaken me?" were the words of your Son as he hung dying on the cross. Sometimes I feel like yelling out the same thing.

Please, God, help me to overcome my fears, troubles, and sorrows. My God, I try my hardest to think, do, and say as you would want me to. But sometimes it's hard, or it doesn't even happen. Sometimes I misbehave, make fun, or call others names. I am sorry for that, and I would like the help of you and your Son to avoid doing those things that have hurt you, others, and even me. In your name I pray.
Amen.

*Matthew Fisher*
*Saint Mary Magdalen School, Altamonte Springs, FL*

God, I am sorry for my sin. I didn't think before making a wrong choice. Please forgive me and wash my sin away. God, I am sorry for the times when I thought you never loved me and were not looking over me. Please be with me every single day, and I'll try to tell that you are here with me. I know how much you love me.

*Xw Thao*
*Saint Bernadette School, Milwaukee, WI*

God, I feel loneliness at school, between classes and at lunchtime. I feel depressed and lonely. I feel like I don't have many friends. When I am at home lying on my bed at night, I feel lonely. I feel depressed and sad whenever I get in a fight with my mom and dad. God, help me always to feel wanted and important. Help me to feel loved.

*D. A. S.*
*Shrine Academy, Royal Oak, MI*

God, please help me through this time, because I just lost a loved one. My heart is broken. But you must know, because you know everything. Guide me through the bad times, and even the mad and angry times. When I stop what I'm doing and I see the first star of the night, I will always think of you. When there is anger in my mind, help me keep it down. I know that sometimes I may forget you at happy times, but I think you are in every happy thing that I do. I love you forever.

*Jessica Watkins*
*Saint John the Baptist Parish, Alvin, TX*

Dear God,
I am not feeling the best that I could right now. That is because my grandma just passed away yesterday. She was very old, and I have a lot of memories of her. Because she was so old, she was always sick, but she always seemed to pull out of it. This time it was too much. I feel sad, but I should be happy that she has a better life now with you. Grandma, please watch over me and help me to make good decisions for the rest of my life.

*Dan Terpening*
*Saint Maria Goretti School, Schiller Park, IL*

Dear God, please listen to how I feel:
Anybody's dream can fall apart.
Anybody's heart can break.
Never knowing what this world will throw at me,
I don't know how much I can take.
I could die today,
so why not live like there's no tomorrow?
Never feeling a prick of pain,
nor an ounce of sorrow.
Never getting a second chance to make a first impression,
I shall feel as if I rule the world,
never wallowing in depression.
In times of need I turn to you,
when all else seems to fade away.
And you alone will help me face the world
with each passing day.
Amen.

*Shannon J. Becknell*
*Saint Stephen School, Pennsauken, NJ*

Dear God,
School is boring and too long. I get bad grades, and I feel like
I'm wasting my valuable time. I can't wait until grade school
is over. I am trying hard to get better grades. And God, I
need your help.

*Brandon Halverson*
*Saint Paul School, Genesee Depot, WI*

In the pitch black of evil,
there could be no hope
without the light of God.

In the damp darkness of the world,
the golden rays of God's love
can still shine through.

Like a tiny match
struck in a darkened room,
God can show us the way.

When the darkness frightens us
and it seems there is no hope in sight,
God's light will give us the courage to go on.

Though evil and hatred may surround us,
the smallest flicker of God's gentle heart
can give us the strength to love.

When we are blind to the goodness in others,
the warmth of God's light
will open our eyes.

In the pitch black of evil,
there could be no hope
without the light of God.

*M. and R.*
*Saint Anthony School, Dayton, OH*

**Why, Grandpa?**

Why did you have to leave?
Your life was so full.
Why did it have to be you
Who suffered body and soul?

Do you still think of me?
Because I still think of you.
I miss you very much.
If you only knew.

How did it happen so quickly?
On that warm windy day,
When you couldn't stop the fire,
It burned your life away.

Why does Grandma seem to suffer now,
Now that you have found your place?
If only she could understand
What it is like to see God's face.

*Anna Reese*
*Saint Mary School, Saint Marys, KS*

Dear God,
When something bad happens, everybody always says, "God wanted it that way." But it doesn't make sense that God would want young, innocent people to be murdered, raped, or kidnapped. If you think about it, God would want us to be happy and to have friends to talk to. Usually, when something bad happens, something good follows. When a door is closed, God always opens a window.

*Melissa Pottebaum*
*Saint Patrick School, Sheldon, IA*

Dear God,

I'm sorry I have not been talking to you. It's been really hectic lately because of this darn separation. It's really hectic moving back and forth from house to house. Other things that are really pulling me apart are my mom's boyfriend and my dad's girlfriend. They both try to act as my parent. I can't picture them as my parent. I just hate it when my dad's girlfriend acts like my mom; it really bugs me. But it is different at my mom's. Her boyfriend just pays too much attention to her, and she pays too much attention to him. I know it sounds selfish, but I think I should be treated the same. One thing my mom does that my dad doesn't do is to be overprotective. So, God, I thank you for listening and for always being there for me. I just needed to get it out of my system.

*Christopher Hayes*
*Saint Hedwig School, Wilmington, DE*

Dear God,

Why do bad things always seem to happen to good people? I know you don't make these things happen, but my grandma is a great person, and she had a stroke. I would like to thank you for taking care of her and the rest of my family and for keeping us healthy and safe. Another thing is that my dad quit his job and finally started a new one, but we will be moving because of his job. I pray that you will keep me strong and help me to make the best of things, even when it seems like things couldn't get any worse.

*Danielle Kobylski*
*Our Lady of Perpetual Help School, Ellicott City, MD*

Dear Jesus,

When times are bad, please give me **hope.**

When times are good, please give me **wisdom.**

When times are sad, please give me **faith.**

And God, please give me **love.**

Amen.

*Matt Lisowski*
*Saint Teresa of Ávila Parish, Norristown, PA*

Dear Jesus,
I know you listen to my prayers and wishes. This prayer isn't for me. It's for my mom. My mom is having a hard time. She is sick and in pain. I was hoping that you'd help her through this time. I know that she loves you and would appreciate it very much. Amen.

*Christine Rebholz*
*Most Holy Name School, Pittsburgh, PA*

O God of wisdom and light,
we come to you broken and sad.
Those who have passed leave without saying good-bye,
which makes us very sad,
and sometimes even mad.
But I know you will help us get through this.
I ask you to give me courage
and to take away my anger, God.

*Johnny Quintana*
*Immaculate Conception Parish, Green River, WY*

★★★

God,
I'm drowned in
sorrow
floods of tears
my heart
with wrenching
fears. . . .

But . . .
I can overcome them with YOU.
I can get over them with YOU.
I can do anything with YOU.
Thank you for loving me.

*Krystal Koros*
*Saint Jude the Apostle School, Westlake Village, CA*


★★★

Dear God,
I look at the sky—
Why do I cry?
Why must people die?
I cry inside
So no one knows.
When the wind blows,
It blows through me
Like a stake through the heart.
Thinking of a reason,
Trying so hard to make the best,
But getting no rest.
When family dies,
All I do is cry.

*Kimberly Lynn Bazzani*
*Saint Hedwig School, Wilmington, DE*

✷✶✷

God,
help me when I'm sick,
rescue me when I'm in danger,
assist me when I need assistance,
tend me when I'm lonely,
give me courage when I'm afraid,
give me wisdom when I'm tempted,
support me when I'm trying something new,
strengthen me when I'm weak and helpless.
Amen.

*Tichelle S. Richards*
*Saint Ann Academy, Washington, DC*


✷✷✶

Dear God,
The world is falling apart.
The older I get, the faster this world tends to spin.
I am getting too dizzy!
The pressure of life is building up.
Pollution clouds *everyone's* vision.
Thoughts of poverty make the heart ache.
Violence is ruining lives.
The demons of greed and hate infest humanity.
Help us, God!
Give your divine inspiration to this generation.
With your guidance I know the children can keep our world
    from spinning out of control.

*Jenny Elizabeth Domine*
*Holy Name School, Racine, WI*

Dear God,
You tell us to

## make peace

with others, but sometimes it's hard.
You help us in times of need.
Help us to love others as Jesus said.

*Jenny Morgen*
*Saint Paul School, Genesee Depot, WI*

Dear God,

When I am sad, hurt, or scared, I look to you,

hoping you will heal me in any way you can.

God, help me to forgive those who hurt me in any way.

To this I say—**Amen.**

*Sonja L. Shirley*
*Saint Mary on the Hill School, Augusta, GA*

God, please forgive me like my best friend forgave me. I shouldn't have asked her to do it, but I did. It got both of us in trouble. It should have been just me in the school office, not my friend. But yet she stood by me. With tears in her eyes, I tried to comfort her. It was the hardest thing to do, except for telling my mom. I said to my friend in a shaky voice, "I'm sorry." She said, with a sniffle and a tear in her eye, "I forgive you." So, God, I'm asking you to do what she did. Please, dear God, forgive me for cheating.

*Jenny Morano*
*Regina Elementary School, Iowa City, IA*

O God,
Times now are hard. Most times I don't know what to do.
I get stressed out easily—mostly over little things. I don't
know where to turn. Everything looks the same.

I want to turn to you, God, but for fear of being laughed
at, I don't. It seems most of your people have turned away.
Still, I hope you continue to care for us who struggle to
remain faithful.

Through your love and care, help us to grow in your
eyes, and help us not to stray.

*Natalie A. Bush*
*Saint Mary on the Hill School, Augusta, GA*

As odd as it may seem, I thank you for the troubles in my life.
It was the hard times in my life that I learned from the most.
From these times I learned courage, strength, and, most of all,
that when it seems that everything in my life has failed, I can
turn to you. It was when my head was down and my heart
was aching that I was truly able to see God in my life. I saw
you in my sister's sweet smile and in my mother's gentle touch
that told me that one day—maybe not today or tomorrow,
but one day—it would be okay. You were with me every step
of the way, and now it is okay. God, it is the trouble and
misfortune in my life that have allowed me to truly appreciate
the happiness you have placed in my life.

*Victoria A. McCardell*
*Cathedral Carmel School, Lafayette, LA*

You see yourself standing in the midst of a highly populated city. On your right you see gang members trying to sell marijuana to an eleven-year-old. On your left you see middle-aged men robbing a jewelry store. And behind you are more gang members stealing a poor old woman's car. Above, the evening sky is full of stars, but the beauty is interrupted by a police helicopter flying around. Down on the ground, police sirens are blaring, signaling trouble. You stand there alone, scared, and you think to yourself, "Is this what life has in store for me?"

*Neilbrian Abellanosa*
*Santa Barbara School, Dededo, GU*

**Prayer of the Scared and Lonely**

O my God, to whom I pray,
will you listen to what I say?
And help me do all that's right,
help me get away from fright.
Please, will you take care of me,
tell everyone to let me be?
Cause I'm lonely, cause I'm scared,
cause I was crying and nobody cared.
O my God, to whom I pray,
please help me get through the next day.

*Michael J. DiGiovanni*
*Saint Francis of Assisi School, Jacksonville, NC*

For all those days
when anger swells
inside my fragile heart
and frustration swallows me whole,
I ask for you to be there.

For all those days
when confusion flows
all through my mind,
when life is a labyrinth, impossible to solve,
I ask for you to be there.

For all those days
when my soul screams out
and I am a prisoner of my own walls,
when all I want is an escape,
I ask for you to be there.

Yes, even when joy rings out from the mountaintops
and the sun is brightest yet,
when all seems right
and my song sings bright,
I ask for you to be there . . .
I need for you to be there.
Amen.

*Meghann M. Hiscocks*
*Saint Jude the Apostle School, Westlake Village, CA*

I stand in a dark room all alone. I do not feel you, but you are there. I do not see you, but you see me. You stand with me when I think I stand alone. I curse you and shake my fist at you, but you love me. I sit and scream at you for being silent, but you are loud. You make a sound in my life, but it's sometimes hard to hear.

*Jaclyn Leigh Broderick*
*Saint Peter School, Huber Heights, OH*

Sometimes I wish it had never happened to her.
But it did.
I thought it was my fault that you left her.
But I knew I was wrong.
God said it was time to go.
You left without warning.
You left my mother sad, thinking about you all the time.
But, I know, at least you can rest in peace.

*Crystal Reynoza*
*Saint John of the Cross Parish, New Caney, TX*

# Part Seven

# Conversations with God

...in heaven
...r my prayer.
...p me in thy loving care.
Be my guide in all I do.
...ss all those who love me too. ...e

courage

...en 1
...mid, and guidance
...ed. And let
...er the

God made many thin...
this world I can...
remembered to m...

God, Please help me throug...
times of good and bad. Ple...
help me think not of w...
vant, but what others ...
Amen

The Lord is my soccer coach;
I get put into the game as much as I need.
He lets me rest on the sidelines of the field.
He gives me the strategy to score a goal.
He guides me past the defensemen, as he promised.
Even when I play in the dark of night, I won't be afraid, for
    you are with me.
Your guiding hand and positioning protect and comfort me.
You give me strength when I play in the game of life and the
    other team is bigger.
You welcome me at practice and fill me up with hope when
    I'm afraid.
I know your helpfulness and love will be with me all my life,
And your field will be my practice area
As long as I live.

*Jason Stasinos*
*Our Lady of Perpetual Help School, Holyoke, MA*

Dear God,
Hi! What's up? Remember me? You know, the girl in the sixth
grade with the little brother. I thought you'd remember me.
Help me to do good on all my schoolwork and to be nice to
everyone in the class (yes, even the boys). Bless my family
and protect them. Keep all the innocent people in the world
safe. Please protect my friends and teachers. Also, please help
all my school's basketball teams to do well in the coming
year. Well, I have to go. Talk to you later.

*Laura*
*Our Lady of Perpetual Help School, Ellicott City, MD*

God,
Why does the sun shine so bright?
Why do the stars twinkle at night?
What makes the trees grow so tall?
Why are flowers so delicate and small?
Why do people have pain and cry?
Why do my loved ones have to die?
Why do some people only want to do wrong?
Do we have to live in fear our whole life long?
I have so many questions, the answers I cannot see.
One thing I know is that you love me.

*Ashley Hofmeister*
*Saint Thomas More School, Omaha, NE*

Dear God,
You have given me everything I need in life.
    I have taken it for granted.
You have given me all that I have ever wanted.
    I am still not satisfied.
You give me loving people in my life.
    I still ask for more.
But most important, you gave me your love,
    and I have used it wrong.
My God, I am sorry with all my heart.
I don't deserve to be forgiven.
    You forgive me anyway.
    You take away all my sins.
And for all these reasons,
    You are my God.

*Erin Filsinger*
*Saint Bernadette School, Milwaukee, WI*

God in heaven,
Hear my prayer.
Keep me in your loving care.
Be my guide in all I do.
Bless all those who love me too.

*Erin DeMoss*
*Saint Ann Parish, Bethany Beach, DE*

Dear God,

Please **help me** through each day.

**Protect me** from all the danger and harm in this world.

With your love, **guide me** to do what's right.

With your Spirit, help me to show joy.

Amen.

*Allison Gossin*
*Saint Louis School, Clarksville, MD*

We believe in God the Father, Jesus Christ, and the Holy Spirit. We ask them to cover us with their protection, to bless us, and to keep our family safe and joyful. Please take away all the guns and crime on our streets, stop the hatred among the people of this world, and give us peace on earth. Help us to remember to have faith in you, God, and to know that you will always be there for us when we need you. Amen.

*Courtney L. Evans, Noah M. Gras, Walter P. Jochum, Sarah E.*
*Moity, Daniel K. Munch, Darryl P. Traylor Jr.*
*Our Lady of Lourdes Parish, Violet, LA*

Dear God,
Summertime, wintertime, and all that's in between
Hold some things we do not notice, some things we do
       not see.
If I take a stormy night where dark clouds fill the air,
I can say I've never realized that a white one's still up there.
And when the grass is snowy white, I'd bet you've never seen
That there's still one blade of grass that tries to keep its green.
In fall the leaves change colors and drop orange, yellow,
       and red.
There's one that still remains there using branches as a bed.
Help me to stop and notice things
And to see the hidden treasures that life brings.

*Lauren Malecki*
*Our Lady of Hope/Saint Luke School, Baltimore, MD*

Jesus, is that really you? Am I really this worthy to meet you
and stand here in your presence? This is truly an honor, and
I feel like God has given me wings, just being here with you.
But I haven't learned to fly yet. I need to talk to you first. Will
you listen? Do you have time to listen to a nothing like me?
I feel like you're the only one who can reach into my darkness
and take me under *your* wing and cleanse me of my sins. I feel
like I'm standing with the whole world on my shoulders, and
you are the only one who can take my sins and frustrations
in this world and carry them on your own shoulders with no
complaints—only love and smiles. Can you take *my* cross
off of my shoulders and let me take off in flight without my
burdens, fears, and sins? Can you teach me how to fly?

*Katie*
*Saint Leonard Faith Community, Dayton, OH*

Dear God,
I have so many questions to ask you. Like, why is the sky blue, or, what do you look like? But why do you stand by me when I'm not nice, or even listen to me? I blame you for a lot, but you are always there for me. You are so far away, but you are close to me in my heart. You are there when I need someone to listen to me. I wish you could talk to me to tell me what you think or to tell me how I could do better. Even though I cannot see you or hear you, I know you are there. You will always be there. When I'm sad or happy or scared, you will be there to guide me through it. Even when I'm dead, you will be there. Maybe then I can see you and hear your words. You have given me so many things, like family and friends who care about me. God, there is no way I could repay you. Thank you so much. I have things that other people don't have that I take for granted. Dear God, thank you.

*Erin Grimm*
*Saint Joseph Middle School, Appleton, WI*

Dear God,
Why does the sun rise?
Why does it set?
Why do some people get things that others don't get?
    I ask all these questions and search for the answers, but you are the answer to all my questions. You make the sun rise. You make it set. You make some people get things that others don't get. You know what's best, and you give us the best, too. God, I like that it's just me and you. Nothing else matters to me because I know that you love me. Amen.

*Clare Cook*
*Cathedral Carmel School, Lafayette, LA*

Dear God,
Today I do not ask for something from you, but instead I wonder what I can do. I feel that too many of my prayers are my asking for specific things from you. But now I am searching for a way to repay all your goodness. As I try every day to follow in your footsteps, I often find many obstacles that keep me from accomplishing this. Overall, the only thing I ask of you is to tell me what I can do to strengthen my relationship with you. I am ready, fully, to serve you the best that I can.
    Love,

*Marybeth Blanton*
*Saint Pius X Parish, Indianapolis, IN*

GOD,
You are light.
You are darkness.
You are earth.
You are sky.
You are black.
You are white.
You are life.
You are death.
You are everything.
AMEN!

*Robert Klein*
*Saint Hilary Parish, Fairlawn, OH*

God, you make it rain for the flowers to bloom. You make the sun shine to make me all warm inside. Every kind of weather has a special kind of meaning to it. Lord God, you are my sun. You brighten up my life. You continue to shine in a lot of different ways. And when I feel lonely, I take a long walk, and somehow I am certain—so very certain—that you are there with me. God, I will walk down your path of trust, love, and care with honor, pride—and with you.

*Robert Bryan*
*Saints Peter and Paul School, Saint Thomas, VI*

Oh God, I know how great and powerful you are, so I praise
     you.
I know how good and just you are, so I thank you.
I know that you have created us all, so I applaud you.
I know that you will keep my best in mind.
For that, God, I love you.

*Tricia Sartor*
*Saint Robert Parish, Flushing, MI*

Give thanks to God with all your heart,
    for God has given you everything that you have.
Love God with all your soul,
    for God has given you everything that you love.
Honor God with all your strength,
    for God has given you the courage to move on with life.
Worship God with all your might,
    for God watches over you all your life.

*Angela Morrison*
*Assumption School, Jacksonville, FL*

Dear God,
I thank you for being here with me. I've questioned what people have told me about you, not knowing what to believe. There are many mysteries, but I've learned that that's what faith is all about. By questioning you, I've shown that I have some belief. I can now see all that you have done for everyone. You created the sunrise over the mountains and the sunset at dusk, the birds and the flowers, and all other beautiful sights. Best of all, you created my brothers and sisters. You must really love us to do all that. Amen.

*Katherine Groff*
*Saint Peter School, Huber Heights, OH*

Dear God,
Please give me **strength** when I need it,
**courage** when I'm afraid,
and **guidance** when I'm confused.
And let your **justice** roll over the earth.

Amen.

*Stephen P. Ferris*
*Columbia Catholic School, Columbia, MO*

Once I was a wandering soul,

among the sin and hate,

but now I have found God in my life.

*Oh, why did I do it so late?*

*Jeffrey Thomas Hausfeld*
*Sacred Heart School, Fairfield, OH*

Dear God,
Everything you created has been touched by your love. You
breathed life into every creature, great and small. With a
sweep of your hand, you sprinkled a fragrance into flowers.
You gave sheep the gift of your gentleness, dogs the gift of
loyalty, lions the gift of bravery, birds the gift of song, and
greatest of all, you created human beings in the image and
likeness of yourself. Help us use our gift in every way possible.
Amen.

*Jenn Chall*
*Saint Louis School, Clarksville, MD*


I stand before the mirror looking at myself,
Seeing myself in retrospect.
I see me good, I see me bad, I see me in between,
But through all these times, good and bad,
You were here with me.

You saw me in my good times, and also in my bad times,
You see my future, you see my past, you see my present
        troubles.
So, help me through this bad time,
Be with me every day.
Please be always at my side, be near me when I pray.

Help the good reflections become reality,
Make the bad ones disappear.
Help me through *all* my times,
Not just the ones I fear.
Amen.

*Melissa Coble*
*Saint Louis School, Clarksville, MD*

If you believe in your heart,
If you believe in your friends,
If you believe in the tall green trees
    and the low grass by your feet,
If you believe in all humanity,
And if you believe in the great big world,
Then you believe in God.

*Caitlin W. Dougherty*
*Saint James Parish, Cazenovia, NY*

God, please help us to become better followers of you.
Give us courage when we are afraid.
Give us strength to withstand persecution.
Give us the willingness to do what is right.
Give us honesty so others will follow you.
Give us faith in hard and troubled times.
Give us hope that we will be with you someday.
Amen.

*Josh Tatel*
*Saint John the Evangelist School, Pensacola, FL*


God Almighty, you are everything in my life.
    You are the sugar in my soda.
    You are the air in my basketball.
    You are the electricity in my Sony Playstation.
Without you I wouldn't and couldn't lead my life.
I need you to instruct and guide me in everything that is right.
I need you to help me make decisions over evil.
Your love is what keeps me going day to day.

*Pat McMahon*
*Saint Bernadette School, Milwaukee, WI*

Dear God,
It's hard to know that you have a best friend that you can talk to and share your feelings with all the time, but you cannot see them. You can hear them if you listen hard enough, but it's usually not the kind of hearing that we know of. Please help me to remember that when my friends are all busy or no one is willing to listen, you will be there to listen, to care, and to love. I hope that I will always be there to listen when someone else needs it and they have not found you yet.

*Jane Votral*
*Our Lady of Light Parish, Fort Myers, FL*

Please, God, watch over me,
### whatever I do,
wherever I go,
### and whatever I say.
Please guide me through it,
### and stick with me.

*Alyssa Behrle*
*Holy Rosary Parish, Ansonia, CT*

God, please help me through times of good and bad. Please help me think not of what I **want** but of what others **need.** Amen.

*Andrea Rau*
*Saint Joseph the Worker School, Beal City, MI*

God, you shower me with love.
God, you bombard me with good fortune.
Let me use this advantage to help others.
Help me fulfill my promises.
Let me be clean-spirited,
free-hearted,
and let me follow in your Son's footsteps.
O God, I praise you!

*Bohdan Kosenko*
*Villa Maria School, Erie, PA*

**The Story of Creation**

God created dark and light,
that are also known as day and night.
On the second day, up real high,
God created the big blue sky.
Also on that day, instead of clutter,
God had to think, and thought of water.

On the third day, there happened to be
a big spot of land and the big blue sea.
In addition to all the seas,
God created the plants and the trees.

The sun was created pretty soon,
and was followed by the stars and the moon.
God created the land so we could be,
and then created all the life in the sea.

When life on earth began,
God decided to create animals and humans.
On the seventh day, the earth was best,
so then God took a big, long rest.

*Robert English, Matthew Gaudette, Tommy O'Connor*
*Saint John Vianney Parish, Cumberland, RI*

Dear God,
In the world there are many obstacles. You are the one who helps us through them.

> You help me to be happy when I am sad,
> feel good about myself when I have no confidence.
> You are a friend when I am lonely.
> You are kind when I am hurt.
> You are loving when my heart is broken.

And most of all, you sent Jesus down to open the gates of
> heaven for us.
For that I am thankful.
Amen.

*Christa Hatch*
*Saint Martin of Tours School, Franklin, WI*

God, you've loved me from the moment of my creation.
You've forgiven me for the things I believed were unforgivable.
You've stood by me during the times when nobody wanted to.
You've shown me miraculous and beautiful things I thought
> were impossible.
You've taught me things a lifetime of experience could never
> teach.
You've given me the gifts of life, love, wisdom, and happiness.
Now that you have done all this, I can return your favor by
> loving, forgiving, standing by, showing, teaching,
> and giving to your people,
as you did for me.

*S. Gabby Knighton*
*Saint Mark School, Catonsville, MD*

GOD,
i know you're there,
always watching,
with me, *in* me.
the knowledge of this *strengthens* me.
i am not afraid.
DIVINE CREATOR,
you do not just give me
what i *want,*
but only what is *best* for me.
in your hands
i place my very *self.*
i know
i can always count on you.
you will never desert me,
though i myself may stray
from your kind and loving presence.
O LOVING GOD,
you are *truly* beyond words.

*Hue*
*De La Salle Academy, New York, NY*

God,
Thank you for always comforting me. You are my sunshine,
my family, my self-value. I find you all around me. You help
me realize that I am worthwhile. You make me happy. You
are the one I can run to without even leaving my seat. You
understand what I want before I begin to tell you. Help me
to stay close to you throughout my life, knowing you are
always reassuring me and cheering me on. You are on my
team, on my side, win or lose. Thank you, God, for always
being there. Thank you, God—for me! Amen.

*Courtney*
*Most Holy Name School, Pittsburgh, PA*

Dear God,

You are the creator of our beautiful earth. You have great power, which we do not fully understand. You have the power to love and to forgive.

We are not all perfect, even though sometimes we think we are. We try hard to love others, but sometimes we just can't. You forgive us. That's what is so great about you.

Sometimes we take things for granted. We should be thanking you for all the gifts and talents you have given us. We should use our special gifts every day.

God, we know that all the prayers we offer will be answered. Sometimes they aren't answered in the way we want, but we trust that you know what's best. Amen.

*James Calenda*
*Saint Joseph School, Sharon, PA*

Dear God,

Sometimes when I think about how you gave your Son for us, an indescribable feeling comes over me. To think that I would be worthy of such a huge sacrifice simply amazes me. But sometimes it makes me feel guilty. Like when I watch the news and hear about people killing each other, and I think to myself that you gave up your Son for people who will turn against you in one way or another and will make millions of mistakes in their life. But I know you see past that. You overlook the negative side we all have and somehow find the smallest amount of love and make it shine through. I am now and will forever be extremely grateful for your sacrifice, which has given me the opportunity to live. Thank you.

*Megan Lee Bianchi*
*Saint Lawrence School, Rochester, NY*

## God made many things in this world.

I cannot believe

## God remembered to make me!

*Mike Young*
*All Saints Parish, Mesa, AZ*

Dear God,

I am not godly, but I am one of your many followers. **Thank you** for my life and the lives of my family.

*C. C. K.*
*Sacred Heart School, Waterloo, IA*

Dear God,
At times when things are going good, I tend to forget you, and I just hope that things stay peachy.

But then a sprained ankle, a sickness, a bad test, and I ask, "Why?! Why did I deserve this trouble? 'So-and-so' is much worse than me!" Then I get mad.

Then I realize it's me I am mad at. I should have zipped up my coat when it was so cold out, I should have studied more for my test, and I realize the "So-and-so's" have their own problems. I also know that the truth is that you are all good and nothing more. Everything that happens has a reason for happening. For all this I thank you. Amen.

*Lauren Weis*
*Saint Columbkille School, Dubuque, IA*

Life is like a roller coaster.
God is my track.
As I go on, God is always with me,
through ups and downs, good times and bad.
God is my future and my past.
I am thankful for the guidance of God's Spirit.

*Joseph Zoccali*
*Saint Joseph Parish, Croton Falls, NY*

Top and bottom,
left and right,
front and back.
I feel safe under your loving gaze,
which watches over me while I am sleeping.

In the morning,
in the hallways at school,
on the way home.
I feel safe.
Your protective gaze watches over me all day long.

Here at home,
far away,
wherever I go.
I feel safe.
Your gaze forever watches over me everywhere I go.

In the morning,
in the afternoon,
late at night.
I feel safe.
Your gaze watches over me all day long.

*Amber Elizabeth Holbin*
*Saint Joseph Parish, Zephyrhills, FL*

God, Almighty Creator of heaven and earth,
I ask you for so many things, like a baby brother or sister,
    safety, forgiveness, help, and so many other petty things.
And I find that you give me help, forgiveness, and love, but
    you don't give me the other things.
I find all those "other things" are material and unnecessary
    for me to have, because I know you love me, and that's
    really all I need.
So, thank you, God, for the things you do give me, and for
    your love.
Amen.

*Ana Martha Strafford*
*Nativity of Our Lady Parish, Darien, GA*

★★★

Life is a miracle, a spindle of love.
My friends are my blessings sent from above.
The earth is a miracle, full of beautiful places
with millions of people of all different races.
People are miracles with smiling faces,
accepting of handshakes and full of embraces.
Thank God for these miracles that walk through each day.
Thank God for faith and the freedom to pray.
Sing praises to our God, the worker of kind deeds.
Preach the words of the sower, for we are the seeds.

*Corinne Noelle Tirone*
*Saint Agnes School, Fort Wright, KY*

If Jesus came to my house,
I'd make some changes fast.
I'd put away the paper plates
And display the plates of glass.

If Jesus came to my house,
I'd ask if he was doing fine.
And everyone would be outside my door,
Trying to form a line.

If Jesus came to my house,
I'd put on my favorite dress.
But with all the people knocking at my door,
I'd never get any rest.

If Jesus came to my house,
I'd give him R-E-S-P-E-C-T.
Not to say I'd suck up,
But I'd want him to like me.

If Jesus came to my house,
I know I'd be excited.
And for him to see how I've improved,
I know he'd be delighted.

*Megan Allen*
*Saint Clare of Montefalco School, Grosse Pointe Park, MI*


Dear God,
I am thankful for the loving family I have, the wonderful
friends I have, and the person I am. Some aren't as lucky as I
am. Always be with me. I will always love you. Amen.

*Ann Marie Locke*
*Saint Michael Parish, Wausau, WI*

## Prayer to the Trinity

Creator God, show me the right path of being loving and kind.
Show me the difference between good and evil.
Help me to reach out to others one day at a time.

Jesus, guide my every step.
Keep me in your heart, and may my love for you increase.
Show me the strength to believe in you and to see your face
    in others.

Holy Spirit, teach me
      to give and receive,
      to respect and love others,
      to break up quarrels,
      and to be a true, loving Christian!!

God, thank you for your faith in me.
Amen.

*Luke J. Collard*
*Mount Saint Joseph Academy, Buffalo, NY*

Dear God, will you always be here for me? I know that there
are billions of other people in the world, but will you always
be here for me? I am trying to take time out of every day to
talk to you. I know that you have been at my side to guide
me throughout my life, but will you continue to be here? You
have done so much for me. You have made me happy, helped
me to make the right decisions, and kept me strong in my
faith. I know that you love me because of who I am, not
because of who I want to be  .  .  .  but will you be here to
guide me when I become that person?

*Matt Larew*
*Regina Elementary School, Iowa City, IA*

God bless the sick who need a cure.
God bless the doctors who can find the cure.

God bless the teens who need guidance.
God bless the parents who can do the guiding.

God bless the kids who need teaching.
God bless the teachers who do the teaching.

God bless your children who love and follow you.
God bless the unbelievers who need you and your love.

God bless those who lead us in prayer.
God bless the people who need to pray.

God bless all your people.
All people need your blessings.
All people need you.

*Carrie Dyer*
*Saint Paul School, Saint Paul, MO*

God, you protect me every day without hesitation.
I have never done anything to deserve this,
but you care for me even when I least think of you.
You have always given me more second chances than
I could ever ask for.
Your reasons are a mystery to me.
The boundaries of your love don't exist.
You and everything about you are beyond anything
I can or ever could comprehend.
And for that I love you all the more.

*T. F. D.*
*Saint Patrick School, Sheldon, IA*

★★★

Dear God,

I know I don't do my best all the time, but when I think of you, I try.

I know I don't follow the rules all the time, but when I think of you, I try.

I know I don't listen to my parents all the time, but when I think of you, I try.

I know I don't help others all the time, but when I think of you, I try.

I know I don't finish my schoolwork all the time, but I thought of you and I finished this.

*Julie Anne Merner*
*Saint Anthony of Padua School, Butler, NJ*

★★★

Dear God,
Sometimes I don't understand you, but I always keep
      believing.
Why do you take family and loved ones from us?
Why do you work the way you do?
I will always believe and love you, God, because I know
      you're there, and you love me, too.
I will never stop wondering, God, and someday I'm sure
      I'll understand the reason you make things the
      way they are.
I know you have a plan.

*Caryn Moskal*
*Our Lady of Light Parish, Fort Myers, FL*

Dear God,
I ask for wisdom and courage and for strength from within me.
I need your help to understand the ups and downs of life.
I need your love to help me through all the pain and strife.
I know I ask a lot of you, but I know I'm very lucky
'cause I have a family and friends and more.
But mostly because I have you.
Amen.

*Christine M. Dever*
*Saint John the Baptist Parish, Lockport, NY*

Thank you, God, for giving me a nice life and parents that
      care about me.
Forgive me, God, for the many times you are not in my
      thoughts, even though you never stop thinking
      about me or loving me.
I trust you to guide me toward the right thing, and I will
      always have faith in you.

*Anthony J. Monte*
*Saint Catherine of Siena School, Metairie, LA*

God, today my teacher talked to me about what would
      happen if I died today.
Sometimes I think about it;
Sometimes I don't because it scares me.
I ask you, if it is my last day, that I use it carefully and wisely,
      like you would.
I thank you for giving me each day to have joy.
Thank you, God, thank you.

*Anne Zagrodnik*
*Saint Mary on the Hill School, Augusta, GA*

For every tear, may there be a smile.
For every fight, may there be an apology.
For every divorce, may there be a marriage.
For every person who hungers, may there be food.
For everyone without a home, may there be shelter.
For every question, may there be an answer.
For every death, may there be life.
For every child, may there be a loving home.
And for everyone who prays, may there be hope.

*Amy Balke*
*Saint Roman School, Milwaukee, WI*

Dear God,

Thank you for . . .

my ears,

my nose,

my eyes,

my mouth,

my fingers,

my toes,

my legs,

my arms,

and also my very special heart.

Thank you, God.

Thank you!

*Claire Holdren*
*Saint Luke Parish, River Forest, IL*

### Bless the Mosquitoes

As I walk along a bumpy road, I think of this wonderful nature,
With all the trees and all the bees and all the furry creatures.
Yet as I walk, I notice this—the mosquitoes seem to be crying.
For they're some pests that never rest,
And are slapped at and always dying.
So as I walk among the dew, I ask you, God,
Please, bless the mosquitoes too!

*Erik J. Richter*
*Saint John Vianney Parish, Brookfield, WI*

God, I know what is the best gift.
    It's not clothes.
    It's not toys.
    It's not games.
    It's not money.
    It's not bikes.
    It's not sports stuff.
It is you.

*Ashley N. McVey*
*Saint Vincent de Paul School, Omaha, NE*

My mysterious Creator, your child is searching for an answer. Your child has looked far and near. He needs your help to find an answer.

"My child, the answer is in you; you just have to find it within yourself."

*T. D. W.*
*Saint Edward Parish, Dana Point, CA*

I love life. It is full of surprises, obstacles, and hardships. None of us would be here today if Jesus hadn't suffered and died for us. The things I love about life are sports, my family, and many other things. I love waking up each day knowing that I can actually enjoy my life. Sometimes I may act wild and crazy, but I am just enjoying life. You may think sports, jobs, school, and other things are really important, but just remember that Jesus is the reason you are here. You wouldn't be here playing sports, working, or doing other things you think are important if it wasn't for Jesus.

*Tye*
*Saint Pius X Parish, Ainsworth, NE*

Blessed Trinity,
You'll always be in my heart.
You brighten each day.

Father, I am blessed.
You bring hope and happiness.
You make my heart live.

Jesus, my Savior,
Embraced in your loving arms,
You make my heart smile.

Oh, Holy Spirit,
Fill me with God's thoughts and love.
You make my heart sing.

*Daniel Lagasse*
*Saint Bridget Parish, North Vassalboro, ME*

When I'm angry, you fill me with your peace.
When I must decide, your spirit guides me.
When I need to forgive, you encourage me.
When I need forgiveness, you listen to me.
When I'm confused, you clarify my problems.
When I'm depressed, you give me joy.
When I'm tired of being good, you give me strength.
When I'm worried, you ease my mind.
When I have forgotten about you, you reveal your presence.
When I want to gossip, you remind me that words can't be
    taken back.
When I'm jealous, you reveal the gifts you blessed me with.

*Amanda Christine Junker*
*Saint Thomas the Apostle School, Phoenix, AZ*


You have taught me everything, and everything you have
given me, I always keep it inside. You kept me up when I was
down. You have given me knowledge to get good grades.
You have always loved and cared for me. You have always
forgiven me when I made the wrong choice and did bad.
You gave me great caring and loving parents. You gave me a
great life. I have all the friends I need. You have given me the
shelter I need. I have great teachers that encourage me to
learn new things every day. You gave me a world to live in.
Without you I would not become a man.

*J. Wesley Harper*
*Saint Francis of Assisi School, Jacksonville, NC*

There is a gift God gave me—the gift of life. I ask God to
help me live it to the fullest.

Let me jump in every creek
      swim in every lake
      sail all seven seas
      reach every mountaintop
      dance in every forest.

Let me walk in every garden
      play in every park
      lay on every beach
      walk every road
      twirl in every meadow.

Let me observe each season
      winter's chill
      autumn's leaves
      spring's flowers
      summer's sun.

Let me watch each sunset with new eyes
      gaze at each star and find its twinkle
      find a new shape in each cloud.

Let me give each ounce of love I have
      breathe each breath as though it were my last
      treasure my friends
      hold my family in my heart
      look for good in every person
And live this awesome life.

*Amy S.*
*Saint Alfred School, Taylor, MI*

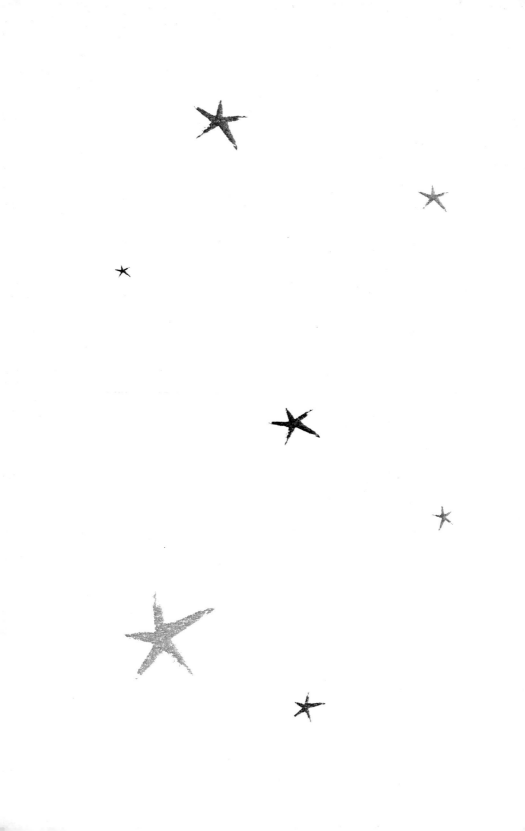

# Index

**Holy Trinity Parish**
Peachtree City, GA
*Sarah Flemings 76*

**Immaculate Conception Parish**
Green River, WY
*Johnny Quintana 105*

**Incarnate Word Academy**
Corpus Christi, TX
*Sally Oelschlegel 56*

**Jackson Catholic Middle School**
Jackson, MI
*Scott Ball 62*
*Kristen Murkowski 80*
*Name Withheld 55*

**Most Holy Name School**
Pittsburgh, PA
*Courtney 127*
*Erin M. Gsell 92*
*Christine Rebholz 105*

**Mount Saint Joseph Academy**
Buffalo, NY
*Luke J. Collard 133*
*Tracy M. Jarvis 25*

**Nativity of Our Lady Parish**
Darien, GA
*Ana Martha Strafford 131*

**Northeastern Catholic Junior High**
Rochester, NY
*Elizabeth Marie Raycroft 29*

**Our Lady of Angels Parish**
Burlingame, CA
*Vince Pivirotto 50*

**Our Lady of Hope/Saint Luke School**
Baltimore, MD
*Rachel E. Cox 30*
*Lauren Malecki 117*
*Kelly McGrath 15*

**Our Lady of Light Parish**
Fort Myers, FL
*Caryn Moskal 135*
*Jane Votral 124*

**Our Lady of Lourdes Parish**
Violet, LA
*Courtney L. Evans, Noah M. Gras,*
*Walter P. Jochum, Sarah E.*
*Moity, Daniel K. Munch,*
*Darryl P. Traylor Jr. 116*
*Candina Rodriguez 13*

**Our Lady of Mercy School**
Rochester, NY
*Christina Chin 45*

**Our Lady of Perpetual Help School**
Ellicott City, MD
*Danielle Kobylski 104*
*Laura 114*

**Our Lady of Perpetual Help School**
Holyoke, MA
*Jason Stasinos 114*

**Our Lady of the Lakes School**
Waterford, MI
*Jessica Sue Wise 82*

**Our Lady of the Rosary School**
Greenville, SC
*Michael Baldwin 44*
*Christy McCuen 93*

**Our Lady of the Sacred Heart Parish**
Lackawanna, NY
*Louis A. DiSarno 91*

**Our Lady of Victory School**
Floral Park, NY
*Ursula Winters 48*

**Our Mother of Sorrows School**
Rochester, NY
*Katherine Cerami 60*

**Precious Blood Parish**
Dayton, OH
*Emily Pilgrim 25*

**Regina Elementary School**
Iowa City, IA
  *Kori Kelly  97*
  *Matt Larew  133*
  *Jenny Morano  108*
  *Theresa Parsons  62*
  *Caitlin Tones  74*

**Roncalli Newman Center Parish**
La Crosse, WI
  *Jacob Thole  72*

**Sacred Heart Parish**
Waynesboro, GA
  *Jonathan Umpleby  94*

**Sacred Heart School**
Bayside, NY
  *Corinne Hartin  17*
  *Erin O'Brien  35*

**Sacred Heart School**
Fairfield, OH
  *Jeffrey Thomas Hausfeld  121*
  *Bryan Scheffel  28*

**Sacred Heart School**
Waterloo, IA
  *C. C. K.  129*

**Saint Agnes School**
Fort Wright, KY
  *John Lorenz  59*
  *Corinne Noelle Tirone  131*

**Saint Agnes School**
Springfield, MO
  *Michelle L. Ciesielski  20*

**Saint Alfred School**
Taylor, MI
  *Amy S.  141*

**Saint Ambrose School**
Houston, TX
  *Tania Castrejón DeOrlow  24*
  *Christopher Navarro Mahoney  14*
  *Aaron Orlando  12*

**Saint Ambrose School**
Rochester, NY
  *Candace R. Holmes  92*

**Saint Andrew the Apostle Parish**
Silver Spring, MD
  *Alexandra Portolano  18*

**Saint Ann Academy**
Washington, DC
  *Virginia J. Jones  82*
  *Tichelle S. Richards  107*
  *Delece Smith-Barrow  54*

**Saint Anne School**
Somerset, WI
  *Peter Adams  89*

**Saint Ann Parish**
Bethany Beach, DE
  *Erin DeMoss  116*
  *Name Withheld  69*

**Saint Anthony of Padua School**
Butler, NJ
  *Heather Ann McKernan  96*
  *Julie Anne Merner  135*

**Saint Anthony School**
Dayton, OH
  *M. and R.  102*

**Saint Bartholomew School**
Bethesda, MD
  *Nick Hamilton-Cotter  44*
  *M. K.  16*
  *Roger Priego  15*

**Saint Bernadette School**
Milwaukee, WI
  *Erin Filsinger  115*
  *Pat McMahon  123*
  *Xw Thao  100*

**Saint Bridget Parish**
North Vassalboro, ME
  *Daniel Lagasse  139*

**Saint Paul School**
Saint Paul, MO
*Carrie Dyer  134*
*Laura Hausladen  21*

**Saint Peter School**
Huber Heights, OH
*Jaclyn Leigh Broderick  111*
*Katherine Groff  121*
*Joe Palmer  55*
*Josh Rankin  71*
*Amy Weatherford  73*

**Saint Peter School**
Lorain, OH
*Ben Kowalczyk  84*

**Saint Philip the Apostle Parish**
El Campo, TX
*Aaron Ermis  73*

**Saint Pius X Parish**
Ainsworth, NE
*Tye  139*

**Saint Pius X Parish**
Indianapolis, IN
*Marybeth Blanton  119*
*Meg Kinney  82*

**Saint Pius X School**
Loudonville, NY
*Frank  44*
*Tanner Holford  71*
*Brendan Lill  43*

**Saint Pius X School**
Tulsa, OK
*David J. Atkins  15*
*Douglas J. Beshara  96*
*Alisha O'Brien  85*

**Saint Raphael the Archangel Parish**
Oshkosh, WI
*Scott Jaworski  56*

**Saint Richard Catholic Community**
Richfield, MN
*Michael  16*

**Saint Robert Parish**
Flushing, MI
*Tricia Sartor  120*

**Saint Robert School**
Shorewood, WI
*Kevin Collins  32*
*Patrick Copps  88*
*Sarah Hoffman  91*
*Ben Howell  64*
*Catherine M. Linn  70*

**Saint Roman School**
Milwaukee, WI
*Amy Balke  137*
*Luke Behnke  36*
*Rebecca Noonan  61*

**Saint Rose of Lima School**
Haddon Heights, NJ
*Sarah Lauren Carmody  75*

**Saints Anthony and Joseph Parish**
Herkimer, NY
*Jim Mula  48*

**Saints Peter and Paul Parish**
New Braunfels, TX
*Eighth-grade CCD class  88*

**Saints Peter and Paul School**
Saint Thomas, VI
*Robert Bryan  120*
*D. A. S.  74*

**Saint Stanislaus School**
Winona, MN
*Susan Marie Bronk  38*
*David D. Miller  53*

**Saint Stephen School**
Pennsauken, NJ
*Shannon J. Becknell  101*
*Maria Orabona  93*

**Saint Teresa of Ávila Parish**
Norristown, PA
*Matt Lisowski  105*

**Saint Theresa School**
Phoenix, AZ
*Jaemi Bowers 22*
*Lindsay D. Martin 98*
*Monique Nuñéz 30*

**Saint Thomas Aquinas School**
Wichita, KS
*Missy L. Dondlinger 43*
*Martin Longhi 83*

**Saint Thomas More School**
Omaha, NE
*Megan Borer 12*
*Ashley Hofmeister 115*
*April Marie Kick 37*

**Saint Thomas School**
Fort Thomas, KY
*Kelly Koeninger 14*

**Saint Thomas the Apostle School**
Phoenix, AZ
*Megan A. Chlarson 54*
*Amanda Christine Junker 140*

**Saint Vincent de Paul School**
Omaha, NE
*Ashley N. McVey 138*
*Lauren Spittler 19*

**Saint Vincent de Paul School**
Rogers, AR
*Ben Blakeman 87*
*Nick J. Peranteau 58*

**Santa Barbara School**
Dededo, GU
*Neilbrian Abellanosa 110*

**Seton Catholic Junior High School**
Houston, TX
*Danielle Coulanges Isles 74*
*Ashley Quintanilla 60*
*Heather Crystal Sowers 75*

**Shrine Academy**
Royal Oak, MI
*D. A. S. 100*
*Ben Tassin 68*
*Parker Turczyn 47*

**Villa Maria School**
Erie, PA
*Star Udell Clark 51*
*Bohdan Kosenko 125*